THE BEST

CRAFT

COCKTAILS

★ ★ ★ ★

& BARTENDING WITH FLAIR

THE BEST
CRAFT
COCKTAILS

★ ★ ★ ★

& BARTENDING WITH FLAIR

**AN INCREDIBLE COLLECTION OF
EXTRAORDINARY DRINKS**

JEREMY LEBLANC, HEAD MIXOLOGIST OF
ALTITUDE SKY LOUNGE **AND CHRISTINE DIONESE**

PAGE STREET
PUBLISHING CO.

PAGE STREET
PUBLISHING CO.

First published in 2013 by
Page Street Publishing Co.
27 Congress Street, Suite 103
Salem, MA 01970
www.pagestreetpublishing.com

Distributed by Macmillan; sales in Canada by The Canadian Manda Group;
distribution in Canada by The Jaguar Book Group.

16   15   14   13   1   2   3   4   5

ISBN-13: 978-1-62414-027-3
ISBN-10: 1-62414-027-0

Library of Congress Control Number: 2013942495

Cover and book design by Page Street Publishing Co.
Photography by Sean Cassidy

Printed and bound in China

*For Ava, Gavin & Milan . . . to the
kaleidoscope of life ahead!*

CONTENTS

★ ★ ★

THE CLASSICS RE-IMAGINED FOR TODAY'S SOCIAL DELIGHTS

★ ★ ★

What exactly is a craft cocktail? Must it be made with herbs? Does it absolutely have to contain gin? To us, a craft cocktail is one that has been constructed with time and thoughtfulness, intended to imprint an unforgettable taste. And in these pages we have done just that. We have compiled an extraordinary collection of cocktails that will bring awareness to the senses in a way you and your guests have yet to experience. Whether you're hosting a party in your own home or you're a mixologist entertaining patrons from behind a bar, you're sure to find a number of recipes here that will excite your taste buds and have your fellow drinkers coming back for more.

In this book, we upped the ante for creating our signature flavor profiles by using fresh organic plants, flowers, herbs and spices. We were flattered to hear from our more experienced taste testers that our selection of these fine ingredients revived their memories of classic cocktail flavors, yet added an updated, more sophisticated, clean taste.

There are so many amazing small-batch spirits that we love, and that's why we spent countless hours naming them in our recipes. Sure, you may not have your hands on one of the smoky Islay peats we chose every time you make the drink, but we encourage you to allow this collection to serve as a guide to expanding your spirits profile beyond the more well-known names and to the world of small-batch spirits. We've included the more familiar names for convenience, but it's also fun and surprising to use more exotic spirits when you can. We also know that people's tastes change, and that is why no aroma, texture or mouthfeel was spared while compiling these recipes. With a mindful approach, we have crafted cocktails that will delight even the most particular guests and drinkers. As you read on, you'll also see that we suggest using Tin Play tins to perfect your mixing, but feel free to use regular tins if you can't get your hands on one.

We know that people drink for myriad reasons. In the end we created these libations to infuse our spirit of adventure into mixologists and party-goers alike. We hope that in no time at all your pages will become dog-eared, you'll have made tasting notes in the margins and there will be drops of booze throughout. We know this collection will get you thinking and will give you the confidence to create a drink that will create regulars at your bar and have friends inviting themselves over to your house for drinks again and again.

Cheers!
Jeremy & Christine

★ ★ ★

THE *APÉRITIF*: TO OPEN THE SENSES

The apéritif: a perfect all-occasion refreshment cocktail to greet one's guests as they arrive to the soirée; a light, polite welcome to the couple or ladies who've just sat down to your bar before dining. Once only regarded as a popular European tradition, our guests happily enjoy warming up to the evening with their favorite apéritif. Learn to amuse your patrons' appetites and they will be sure to find a regular seat at your bar.

Meant to heighten the senses and stimulate appetite, these herbal-based cocktails will naturally encourage mingling and set the social tone of the evening. Focusing attention on drier spirited liquors and liqueurs is essential to making these drinks a success. Allow herbal elements such as citrus peel, anise, gentian, juniper and sage to speak for themselves. A champagne with a hint of Lillet Blanc will exude your prowess of the fine art of apéritif preparation. Keep it simple, keep it dry; save the sweeter things for après le dîner.

A well-stocked mixologist is always ready to appeal to the taste of all guests. Your more familiar selections of apéritif of course include Campari, Lillet Blanc, Dubonnet, vermouth and fino sherry. Perhaps more obscure, yet noteworthy and sure to pique the interest of guests when offered, we love Armenian Ararat, Italian Dimmi and cider from Quebec.

Let's start the night off right!

JAMAICAN DREAM

★ ★ ★

THE JAMAICAN DREAM IS AN IDEAL CHOICE BEFORE EATING A HEARTY
MAIN COURSE. RUM FROM JAMAICA UNITES WITH HIBISCUS LIQUEUR
TO TOP OFF YOUR BUBBLES. WITH AN INITIAL CLEAN AND CRISP TASTE,
THE LONG FINISH OF THE RUM'S COMPLEXITY WILL OF COURSE
HAVE GUESTS ORDERING ANOTHER.

YIELDS 1 APÉRITIF

---

3 oz/90 ml Champagne Brut

1 oz/30 ml Jamaican rum (we like Extra Old Mezan Rum for this recipe)

1 oz/30 ml hibiscus liqueur (we like Fruitlab Hibiscus Organic Liqueur
for this recipe)

To make the dream come true, be sure your brut is cold, cold, cold. In a thin
champagne flute, layer in rum and champagne. Appeal to your guest's eye
by circling the rosy hibiscus liqueur over the top of their bubbles.

THE JADE CLOUD

★ ★ ★

THE JADE CLOUD IS OUR FAVORITE APÉRITIF. GIVEN ITS NAME
BECAUSE OF ITS ALLURING CLOUD-LIKE HUE, THIS REFRESHMENT WILL
BRIGHTEN YOUR GUESTS' EYES AND GET THEM TALKING. THE HIBISCUS
BITTERS BRING THE ORGANIC WHITE TEA AND LILLET BLANC ALIVE
IN THIS DELICIOUS COCKTAIL.

YIELDS 1 APÉRITIF

---

1 oz/30 ml organic white tea

3 oz/90 ml purified water

6 small ice cubes

2 oz/60 ml Lillet Blanc

2 dashes white hibiscus bitters

Dry ice (optional)

First things first: brew the white tea to steep a rich, bold flavor. Brew one
tea bag or 1 ounce/30 milliliters loose-leaf tea in 3 ounces/90 milliliters of
purified water. If a tea bag has been used, press remaining liquid
into your brewing vessel.

Slowly stir in six small cubes of ice, allowing tea to reach room temperature.
Pour 1 ounce/30 milliliters into the bottom of a shaker without ice.

Pour Lillet Blanc into the middle of the shaker. Add your bitters and stir.
Now it's time to pour that mixture into your glass of ice, slowly, like
a circular waterfall.

We love to add an extra dash of bitters to slowly melt through the ice. To add a
little flair as guests arrive, consider adding dry ice to personify the Jade Cloud's
character. Drop one dry ice chip into your cocktail after it has been built and
garnished. Encourage guests to sip slowly if dry ice is added.

VAPEURS

★　★　★

INSPIRED BY A WINEMAKER FROM ITALY WHO ONCE INVITED US FOR A TASTING,
VAPEURS PAYS HOMAGE TO A LESSER-KNOWN NORTHERN ITALIAN SPIRIT, DIMMI.
ON THE FIRST SIP YOU'LL TASTE VANILLA AND LICORICE, WHICH WILL QUICKLY BE
EXCHANGED FOR AN EARTHIER GINSENG. JUST AS YOU'RE THINKING ABOUT THIS
INTERESTING ARRANGEMENT OF FLAVOR, THE MORE FLORAL APRICOT BLOSSOM
WILL ARISE TO THE OCCASION. DIMMI IS INFUSED WITH ASSENZIO GENTILE,
AN ITALIAN ABSINTHE, SO BE SURE TO POLITELY TELL GUESTS WHY
ONLY ONE WILL DO THE TRICK.

YIELDS 1 APÉRITIF

Shaved ice

2 oz/60 ml Dimmi Liquore di Milano

1 oz/30 ml pisco

2 dashes black walnut bitters (Fee Brothers makes a great one)

Pack one small glass with a mountainous pile of ice. In your shaker, pour Dimmi
and pisco. Stir for 30 counts, allowing the exotic arrangement of flavors to
marry. Slowly pour around the edge of the glass finishing in the middle. To the
remaining ice add bitters and give the drink one swirl of the wrist.

AU CANADA

★ ★ ★

CIDER HAS MADE A RECENT REVIVAL INTO CRAFT COCKTAIL CULTURE.
OUR FAVORITE HAILS FROM QUEBEC AND IS A SPECIAL APÉRITIF VARIETY.
WHEN COMBINED WITH JUST A DROP OR TWO OF CHILI OIL AND
SMOOTHED OVER WITH LAVENDER SYRUP, THIS APÉRITIF IS SURE
TO STIMULATE THE GASTRIC JUICES!

YIELDS 1 APÉRITIF

½ oz/15 ml lavender syrup

1–2 drops of red chili oil

3 oz/90 ml cider (we like Union Libre apéritif cider for this recipe)

1 small sprig of fresh French lavender for garnish

In a chilled tumbler, drizzle lavender syrup along the sides and bottom of
the glass. Into the center bottom of your glass, add 1–2 drops of chili oil, taking
care to not create splash. For ideal infusion of flavors, hold tumbler slightly
to its side and pour cider circularly. Garnish with a sprig of lavender
and encourage guests to swirl it about.

THE SPARKLING LAURA

★ ★ ★

INSPIRED BY THE EARLY MORNING SPIRIT OF KIMPTON'S CULINARY GODDESS, LAURA, HENRIOT IS OUR CHOICE FOR BOTH A DRY AND ROSY BUBBLY. BOTH GRAPEFRUIT AND GINGER ENLIVEN THE SENSES ALL WHILE READYING THE PALETTE FOR EARLY DAY DINING.

YIELDS 1 APÉRITIF

3 freshly squeezed grapefruit wedges

3 oz/90 ml rose champagne (we like Henriot Rose Brut Souverain for this recipe)

1 oz/30 ml ginger liqueur (we like Domaine de Canton for this recipe)

What do we drink Sparkling Lauras out of? Why, sparkly glasses of course! In a crystal glass, squeeze the juice of your grapefruit slices. Slowly pour champagne and finish with ginger liqueur before handing off to guests.

THE VICEROY'S WIFE

★ ★ ★

A PLAY ON THE PRE-PROHIBITION FAVORITE, THE VICEROY. WE LIKE TO SAY
THAT THE VICEROY'S WIFE WAS MORE COLORFUL AND FANCIED HERSELF A
MORE FESTIVE DRINK THAN HER HUSBAND. WHILE LILLET BLANC IS CHOSEN
FOR THE VICEROY, LILLET ROUGE'S MELANGE OF CABERNET SAUVIGNON
AND MERLOT ADD ROBUST DEPTH TO THE VICEROY'S WIFE.

YIELDS 1 APÉRITIF

---

2 oz/60 ml pisco

1 oz/30 ml Lillet Rouge

Juice of ½ lemon

1 oz/30 ml tonic water

Small ice cubes

Your guests will love watching you layer this beauty. Oh so gently pour pisco
into the bottom of a skinny champagne flute to avoid splash. Continue by
pouring Lillet, then lemon juice into the glass. Top with tonic and 3–5 small
cubes of ice before serving your guests.

MARTINEZ

HAVEN'T HEARD OF THIS GEM? THE MARTINEZ IS THE EARLY PREDECESSOR
TO WHAT WE SERVE AS TODAY'S CLASSIC MARTINI. TO REDUCE THE SWEETER
TONES THE MARTINEZ IS KNOWN FOR, YET STILL OFFER ITS SIGNATURE
COMPLEX TASTE, WE CHOSE URBAN MOONSHINE'S CITRUS BITTERS.

YIELDS 1 APÉRITIF

1¾ oz/52 ml dry gin (we like Bombay Sapphire for this recipe)
¾ oz/22 ml sweet vermouth (we like Noilly Prat for this recipe)
½ oz/15 ml maraschino liqueur

2 dashes citrus bitters (we like Urban Moonshine for this recipe)
Orange peel for garnish

In a bar tin, stir gin, vermouth, maraschino and bitters for 15 counts.
Strain contents into a chilled coupe. Gently squeeze and twist your peel
to express the oils. Serve with peel along the rim.

TANJEEN NEGRONI

★ ★ ★

OUR NEGRONI APÉRITIF REPLACES THE MORE TRADITIONAL SWEET
VERMOUTH WITH TANGERINE JUICE TO ALLOW THE TRUE FLAVORS OF
CARDINAL GIN TO FLY. WITH HEAVY JUNIPER UPON THE FIRST SIP BUT MINT
ON THE FINISH, THE TANJEEN NEGRONI IS A CRISP CHOICE TO SERVE GUESTS
BEFORE A MEAL THAT INCLUDES MEAT SUCH AS DUCK OR LAMB.

YIELDS 1 APÉRITIF

---

2 oz/60 ml gin (we like Cardinal for this recipe)

½ oz/15 ml Campari

1 oz/30 ml freshly squeezed tangerine juice

Ice

1 thinly sliced tangerine for garnish

In a bar tin combine gin, Campari and tangerine juice. Add 20 pieces of ice
(or 1 scoop of a 16-ounce/475-milliliter shaker) and continuously stir for a count
of 90. Rim a chilled glass with your tangerine slice, strain the contents of your
tin into the glass and serve with the slice to garnish.

PIMM'S ROYAL CUP

★ ★ ★

GUESTS FANCY A CELEBRATORY COCKTAIL TO KICK OFF A SPECIAL
OCCASION? TREAT THEM TO THE SHAVED ICE VERSION OF THIS CLASSIC.

YIELDS 1 APÉRITIF

Shaved ice

1½ oz/45 ml Pimm's No. 1

2 oz/60 ml champagne

Lemon peel

1 cucumber wheel

In a highball glass, create a somewhat overflowing display of shaved ice.
Lift your bottle of Pimm's up high and pour to cascade over the shaved ice.
As you pour, watch the ice gently melt a touch—this will allow the perfect
amount of room to top with champagne. Give the lemon peel a squeeze to
release a bit of the citrus oil to meet a guest's first sip. Garnish with
a cucumber wheel and lemon peel.

PEPPER'S READY

★ ★ ★

THINK CRISP AND CLEAN, YET EXOTIC ENOUGH TO PUT THE BLUSH IN
YOUR CHEEK. THIS APERITIF COULD BE ENJOYED BEFORE A LATE BREAKFAST,
BRUNCH OR DINNER ON A HOT SUMMER NIGHT. WHILE THE FLORAL NOTES
OFFER RELAXATION, THE PEPPERCORN WILL KEEP YOUR
SENSIBILITIES ENLIVENED.

YIELDS 1 SMALL APÉRITIF

---

3 red peppercorns

Ice

2 oz/60 ml gin

1 oz/30 ml Lillet Blanc

½ oz/15 ml rosewater

In your mortar and pestle or in a dry Tin Play shaker, gently muddle
peppercorns in a circular motion to crack open, taking care not to smash them.
Continue muddling until semi-fine granules remain. In your shaker, add
20 pieces of ice (or 1 scoop from the Tin Play 16-ounce/475-milliliter shaker, or
cheater tin), peppercorns (if cracked in a mortar and pestle), gin, Lillet Blanc
and rosewater. With the top left off, swirl your shaker round and round for
five twists of the wrist. Why not shake? The cylindrical rotation created by the
twists will fold the pepper into the rosewater so as not to over-entice a
guest's senses, yet it will provide enough aroma to heighten awareness
and warm the mood.

SHAKE, SHAKE TWIST

★ ★ ★

IT'S ALL IN THE NAME. OBSCURE AS THE INGREDIENTS MAY BE, OUR END OF THE WEEK DINNER GUESTS ARE CLAMORING FOR THE SHAKE, SHAKE TWIST. WHEN PROPERLY EXECUTED, THIS APÉRITIF WILL INCREASE YOUR GUEST'S ALERTNESS SO MUCH THAT THEY MAY BE INSPIRED TO START DANCING BEFORE DINNER. AT THE FIRST SIP, A GROUNDING EARTHY TONE OF ARTICHOKE FROM THE CYNAR IS ESTABLISHED. ANOTHER SIP LIBERATES THE ROSEMARY TO ENERGIZE THE MIND.

YIELDS 1 SMALL APÉRITIF

Ice

2 oz/60 ml Cynar liqueur

1–2 sprays rosemary elixir (we like Mountain Rose for this recipe)

2 dashes lemon zest

Lemon twist for garnish

Combine 20 pieces of ice (or 1 scoop of a 16-ounce/475-milliliter shaker), Cynar, rosemary elixir and zest in a Boston shaker. Ready? Shake once, shake twice, pour through a coupe into a small, delicate glass and voilà. Meant to add just enough chill, the one, two shake will crisp this apéritif without watering down the spirit-lifting rosemary and zest. Float lemon twist on top of apéritif.

SAGELY SPOKEN

★ ★ ★

WHO SAYS SLOE GIN IS ONLY A THING OF THE PAST? WE THINK EVERY
BAR SHOULD BE GRACED WITH AT LEAST ONE FINE BOTTLE. OUR PICK IS
SIPSMITH'S. WHEN COMBINED WITH VELVETY SAGE, THIS SAVORY APÉRITIF
SPEAKS FOR ITSELF. IDEAL FOR THE GUEST WHO PREFERS
A LESS BITTER PREPRANDIAL.

YIELDS 1 APÉRITIF

---

5 fresh sage leaves

3 oz/90 ml Sipsmith sloe gin

3 pieces of cubed ice for stirring

Shaved ice

1 oz/30 ml tonic

Fresh sprig of sage for garnish

In a shaker, tear and gently bruise sage leaves to release the oils. Pour sloe gin
and 3 cubes of ice into shaker, stirring for a moment until the scent of sage hits
the air. In a glass filled with shaved ice, pour apéritif, leaving room for the
tonic topper. Garnish with a sprig of sage to nibble on.

CRACKING GOOD

★ ★ ★

THE VERSATILITY OF SHERRY IS OFTEN OVERLOOKED, YET SHOULD NOT
GO UNDERESTIMATED BEHIND THE MODERN BAR. HERE, ITS ABILITY TO
CAPTURE CREAMY HAZELNUT AND STRONG COFFEE NOTES WILL TAKE
EACH SIP TO A RICH DEPTH. NEW TO SHERRY? CONSIDER LUSTAU—SURE
TO PLEASE A VARIETY OF PALATES.

YIELDS 1 SMALL APÉRITIF

½ tsp coarsely ground coffee

5 shelled hazelnuts

Ice

3 oz/90 ml sherry (we like Lustau Sherry for this recipe)

Get your muddling hand ready for this one. In a dry Boston shaker or with a
mortar and pestle, steadily muddle your dry ingredients to crack open and
marry the oils. A toasted aroma will signal you've achieved proper muddling.
Set aside. In another shaker, add 20 pieces of ice (or 1 scoop of a 16-ounce/
475-milliliter shaker), add sherry and give one shake, add dry ingredients and
shake for an additional 20 seconds. Strain and pour chilled sherry
for a cracking good apéritif.

ARARAT SIPPER

★ ★ ★

THIS BUTTERY ARMENIAN BRANDY IS WORTH EVERY SWIRL IN YOUR SNIFTER. WITH EACH TURN OF THE WRIST, JASMINE AND CITRUS MEET THE SENSES JUST AS THE SIPPER HITS YOUR LIPS TO ENJOY A TASTE. A PERFECT CONVERSATION STARTER TO INTRODUCE NEW GUESTS OR A COUPLE ON A BLIND DATE! WANT TO INFUSE THE FLORAL AND CITRUS NOTES MORE DEEPLY? REST SNIFTER ON ITS SIDE FOR SEVERAL MINUTES OR UNTIL YOU CATCH THE SCENT IN THE AIR.

YIELDS 1 APÉRITIF

1 drop jasmine essential oil

2 oz/60 ml Ararat brandy

Orange zest

In a brandy snifter, place your drop of jasmine in the bottom of the glass. To the top and from a good angle, pour Ararat in one steady stream. Float 2 dashes of zest to the top of the Ararat while giving the snifter a masterful swirl. Rest snifter on its side to allow a deeper infusion of jasmine and citrus.

HELLO YOU

★ ★ ★

HAS MEZCAL MADE ITS WAY ONTO YOUR BAR SHELF YET? IF NOT,
IT SHOULD. YOU WILL WANT TO MIX IT FOR EVERY DROOPY GUEST WHO
PULLS UP A BAR STOOL AS A POLITE WAY OF OFFERING TO TURN THAT
FROWN UPSIDE DOWN. HELLO YOU WILL GENTLY BRING ON A SMILE. FOR THIS
APÉRITIF, WE SELECTED MANO NEGRA FOR ITS GRASSY YET EXOTIC TASTE.
EXPECT THE SIGNATURE SMOKY FINISH MEZCAL IS KNOWN FOR.

YIELDS 1 APÉRITIF

Ice

1 tsp raw honey

2 drops rosemary elixir

3 oz/90 ml mezcal (we like Mano Negra for this recipe)

1 sprig of rosemary for garnish

In a thin, short glass filled to the top with ice, drizzle honey, covering every last
inch of the glass base. Drop in your rosemary elixir and vigorously stir to infuse
the honey. Quickly stirring will bring the minty volatile oils of rosemary into the
glass while allowing the earthier elements to remain infused within the honey.
It's time to add the mezcal, but pour from the bottle straight down into the
center of the glass. No need to stir, simply swirl about three twists of the wrist.
Your guest will be revived simply by the scent of earth and rich smoke.
Garnish with rosemary sprig.

ASHRAM

ENTER AN ASHRAM AS YOU ARE, LEAVE A CHANGED PERSON. AND
THAT IS EXACTLY THE EXPERIENCE THIS MIND-OPENING APÉRITIF EVOKES.
NO BARTENDER IS NEW TO THE GUEST TRAVELING ALONE OR THE QUIET,
CONTEMPLATIVE TYPE AT THE BAR. IF ASKED FOR A RECOMMENDATION, SEIZE
THE OPPORTUNITY TO CRAFT THE ESSENCES OF NAVALINO ORANGE PEELS,
INDONESIAN CASSIA BARK AND CLOVES FROM SRI LANKA WITH
THE MIND-CLARIFYING EFFECTS OF BERGAMOT ESSENTIAL OIL.

YIELDS 1 APÉRITIF

**3 oz/90 ml Scotch whisky (we like Compass Box Orangerie Infusion
for this recipe)**

1 oz/30 ml Dubonnet

1 drop bergamot essential oil (optional; we like NHR Organic Oils for this recipe)

Ice

1 small twist for garnish

In a tin, combine Scotch whisky, Dubonnet and essential oil, stirring for a count
of 30. Strain and pour into a chilled glass full of ice. Allow twist to float. For an
extra-aromatic edge, consider a drop of bergamot essential oil. Engage guest
in conversation about the flavor profile.

★ ★ ★

CLASSICS WITH A TWIST

Our collection of classics affectionately dotes on once iconic cocktails
that were created and enjoyed throughout the pre- and post-prohibition eras.
They've been inspired by timeless anecdotes referencing the hey-day of yester-
year coupled with the many stories our guests have shared in our homes and
at our bars. Here you'll have the opportunity to experiment with a vast array of
flavor profiles that will pleasantly surprise you, perhaps furrow your brow for a
moment here and there and even inspire you to create your own personal twist.

For the twists we've created on these classics, we bring together spirits of
the past and present to feature the highest quality flavor profiles possible.
Tinkering with recipes is welcome, for mixing masterfully is all about
pleasing the tastes of the guest before you.

And to start, what's a better classic than the Manhattan?

THE MANHATTAN

★ ★ ★

WHILE THERE ARE MANY DIFFERENT INTERPRETATIONS, A FEW CONSISTENT MUST-HAVES REMAIN WITH THE CONSTRUCTION OF THE MANHATTAN. GUESTS WILL APPRECIATE THE CARE YOU TAKE TO CREATE THIS TIMELESS CLASSIC WITH A BIT OF FLAIR. WHAT MATTERS MOST HERE? THE PROOF OF YOUR WHISKEY. A WHISKEY WITH A PROOF OF 90–110 IS YOUR TARGET.

YIELDS 1 COCKTAIL

---

2 oz/60 ml rye whiskey (we like Hudson Manhattan for this recipe)

1 oz/30 ml sweet vermouth (we like Martini & Rossi for this recipe)

3 dashes of bitters (we like Fee Brothers for this recipe)

Ice

1 lemon twist

1 maraschino cherry

The coupe is our favorite vessel for serving the Manhattan.
Chill this glass ahead of time.

In a mixing glass, add the whiskey and vermouth. To this, add 3 hearty dashes of bitters. Now, to crack your ice. We crack ice to allow an even, balanced chill. To get a clean crack, place the ice cube in either a clean hand or lint-free bar towel. In your opposing hand, grasp a twisted-handle bar spoon by the very end of the handle and with a firm snap of the wrist, strike ice with the bowl of the spoon. Three to four cracks should do the trick. Now crack 3 more cubes of ice. Place all ice into your mixing glass.

The Manhattan is a classic we stir to create a velvety mouthfeel. After stirring, pull your coupe from the freezer, place in front of your guest onto your bar mat and carefully strain the drink through a traditional julep strainer into your glass. Express the oils from a twist just before serving and add a cherry to get your guest licking their lips.

SEARED PEACH OLD FASHIONED

★ ★ ★

BEST ENJOYED AS AN AFTER-DINNER DELIGHT, SEARED PEACH CREATES A RATHER SMOKY-SWEET SPRINGTIME OLD-FASHIONED. THIS TIME YOU CAN SKIP THE SUGAR BY MUDDLING FRESH PEACH WITH AGAVE NECTAR. TO RETAIN THE NEATNESS OF THE BOURBON, WE INVITE THYME TO THE MUDDLING PROCESS.

YIELDS 4 SMALL COCKTAILS

---

2 ripe yellow peaches

1 tsp blue agave nectar

3 sprigs thyme

4 dashes of bitters

2 tbsp/30 ml squeezed lime

8 oz/240 ml bourbon (we like Willett Bourbon for this recipe)

Ice

With a very sharp knife quarter peaches, setting aside 3 slices to muddle.

In your Tin Play shaker, slowly muddle 3 peach slices, agave, thyme, bitters and lime juice. Add bourbon and divide among four ice-filled glasses. Garnish with peach section and thyme sprigs.

If you have access to a grill or cast iron skillet, sear the peaches set aside for garnish to create a smoky complement.

THE CRAWLING MILAN

★ ★ ★

A VARIATION OF A CLASSIC MILANESE NEGRONI. THIS STIMULATING
COMBINATION OF WHISKEY AND CAMPARI IS ENRICHED WITH FRESH-PRESSED
KUMQUAT. CAMPARI WAS ORIGINALLY COLORED WITH A CARMINE DYE
DERIVED FROM CRUSHED COCHINEAL INSECTS, WHICH GAVE THIS SPIRIT ITS
DISTINCTIVE RED COLOR. WHILE THE ORIGINAL PRACTICE HAS BEEN LEFT
TO THE PAST, THIS TANGY MARTINI DOES HAVE A TENDENCY
TO CRAWL DOWN ONE'S THROAT!

YIELDS 1 COCKTAIL

Ice

1 oz/30 ml Campari

1 oz/30 ml whiskey

½ oz/15 ml sweet vermouth

½ oz/15 ml kumquat juice

1 splash of soda water

3 kumquats for garnish

In a bar tin, add 20 pieces of ice (or 1 scoop of a 16-ounce/475-milliliter shaker),
combine Campari, whiskey, vermouth, juice and splash of soda. Shake
vigorously for a count of 20. Strain and pour into a chilled martini
glass and garnish with 3 kumquats un-submerged.
Encourage nibbling between sipping.

BASIL JULEP

★ ★ ★

A DERBY AND SOUTHERN STAPLE. PERHAPS A MORE SUBTLE VERSION OF ITS COUSIN, THE MINT JULEP, THIS COOL BITE OF WHISKEY IS BALANCED BY THE EARTHY FLAVOR OF BASIL. BEST ENJOYED WITH FRIENDS.

YIELDS 4 SMALL COCKTAILS

---

8 basil leaves, plus 4 for garnish

2 oz/60 ml lime syrup

6 oz/180 ml Irish whiskey (we like Jameson for this recipe)

Crushed ice

In a dry bar tin, muddle 8 basil leaves with the lime syrup. Pour in whiskey and stir this mixture for two revolutions. Prepare four julep glasses with a mountain of crushed ice. Pour equal parts into each glass and garnish with remaining basil. Take in the earthy scent before sipping.

We prefer the slightly sweet notes of Jameson whiskey to perfect this cocktail.

ROB ROY

★ ★ ★

MUCH LIKE THE MANHATTAN, THIS SWEETER VERSION POPPED ONTO THE CLASSIC COCKTAIL MAP AFTER BEING CREATED AT THE FAMOUS WALDORF ASTORIA IN NEW YORK. WHEN A GUEST ORDERS A ROB ROY OR IF THEY LOVE SCOTCH BUT WOULD LIKE A TOUCH OF SWEETNESS, IMPRESS THEIR TASTE BY CRAFTING THIS TWIST ON A TIMELESS CLASSIC. THE CUCUMBER? IF IT'S JUST A TOUCH TOO SWEET AFTER SIPPING, A NIBBLE OF CUCUMBER WILL BALANCE OUT FLAVOR COMPOSITION AND SET YOU BACK TO SIPPING.

YIELDS 1 COCKTAIL

1½ oz/45 ml Scotch whisky

¼ oz/7 ml sweet vermouth

1–2 dashes bitters (we like Fee Brothers for this recipe)

Ice

Maraschino cherries for garnish

1 cucumber slice

In a bar tin, pour Scotch whisky, vermouth and bitters over 20 pieces of ice (or 1 scoop of a 16-ounce/475-milliliter shaker). Shake well for a count of 15. Strain and pour into a well-chilled martini glass. Garnish with your cherries and crisp cucumber slice, telling guests about the added touch.

If your guest has time to settle in, prepare half the suggested recipe and serve two fresh mini-cocktails. So many cocktails become wilted with ice or subdued by the sweeter elements. The Rob Roy is a perfect choice to prepare as a mini-cocktail. Simply let a guest know you'll be by to refresh their glass just as soon as they enjoy their current sipper.

BLOODY MARY

★ ★ ★

ALL HOURS ARE GOOD HOURS OF THE DAY TO ENJOY THIS BURST
OF SMOKE, SALT AND SPICE SANS VODKA. FEATURING LAPHROAIG FRONT
AND CENTER WITH OUR HOMEMADE SAVORY BLOODY MARY MIX WILL
HAVE YOU ORDERING IT THIS WAY EVERY TIME.

YIELDS 1 COCKTAIL

---

2 oz/60 ml Laphroaig single malt whiskey

5 oz/150 ml homemade savory Bloody Mary mix (see page 201)

1 dash horseradish

1 dash chili oil

Ice

Celery for garnish

Pickled green beans for garnish

1 lime wedge and black pepper for rim (optional)

Mix the whiskey and bloody mix in a Boston shaker full of ice. Stir in
horseradish and chili oil. Shake for a count of 20. Strain in a highball glass or
pint glass packed with 20 pieces of ice (or 1 scoop of a 16-ounce/475-milliliter
shaker). Garnish with celery and pickled green bean. Black pepper for glass rim
is optional. To rim glass beforehand, rub lime along rim and dip into
a plate of black pepper.

THE 21ST CENTURY

★ ★ ★

KEEPING IN TUNE WITH THE ORIGINAL COCKTAIL, THE 20TH CENTURY,
WE BRING TOGETHER GIN AND A DOLLED UP VERSION OF WHAT HINTS AT
WHITE CHOCOLATE, ORIGINALLY IMBUED WITH WHITE CRÈME DE COCOA.
AN UNCOMMON FLAVOR PROFILE AT FIRST GLANCE, A STAPLE TO
YOUR "REGULAR" ORDER AFTER THE FIRST SIP.

YIELDS 1 COCKTAIL

1½ oz/45 ml dry gin (we like Gordon's Dry Gin for this recipe)

½ oz/15 ml Lillet Blanc

¼ oz/7 ml freshly squeezed lemon juice

2 dashes chocolate bitters (we like Fee Brothers Aztec for this recipe)

1 tsp vanilla syrup

Ice

1 tsp powdered sugar

Combine gin, Lillet Blanc, juice, bitters and vanilla syrup in a Boston
shaker and 20 pieces of ice (or 1 scoop of a 16-ounce/475-milliliter shaker).
Shake vigorously for a count of 20, strain and pour into a martini glass
or coupe. Stir in powdered sugar and serve this tangy libation.

THE LAST WORD

★ ★ ★

IT'S WHAT LUCID DREAMS ARE MADE OF. PUNGENT AND CLEAN, THE LAST WORD WILL CLEAR YOUR MIND AND CLEANSE THE PALATE. NO COCKTAIL BIBLE OR MIXOLOGIST'S BAG OF TRICKS COULD BE COMPLETE WITHOUT PERFECTING ONE OF OUR FAVORITE CLASSIC COCKTAILS.

YIELDS 1 COCKTAIL

¾ oz/22 ml dry gin (we like Gordon's Dry Gin for this recipe)

¾ oz/22 ml Chartreuse Green VEP

¾ oz/22 ml maraschino liqueur (we like Luxardo for this recipe)

¾ oz/22 ml freshly squeezed lime juice

Ice

In a bar tin, combine gin, Chartreuse, maraschino liqueur, juice and 20 pieces of ice (or 1 scoop of a 16-ounce/ 475-milliliter shaker). Shake well for a count of 20. Strain and pour into a coupe. Serve with a smile.

BLUE MOON

★ ★ ★

WE LIKE IT AS THE CREATOR, HUGO ENSSLIN, INTENDED IT TO BE DRUNK.
SERVE THIS ONE RED BY TOPPING WITH YOUR FAVORITE BORDEAUX-STYLE
WINE AS ENNSLIN DID, AND YOU'LL UNDERSTAND WHY AS YOU SIP.

YIELD 1 COCKTAIL

Ice

2 oz/60 ml dry gin (we like Bombay for this recipe)

1 oz/30 ml dry vermouth (we like Noilly Prat for this recipe)

1 dash orange bitters (we like Fee Brothers for this recipe)

1 dash violet liqueur (we like Bitter Truth for this recipe)

¼ oz/7 ml Claret

1 lemon peel

In a Tin Play tin, add 20 pieces of ice (or 1 scoop of a 16-ounce/475-milliliter
cheater tin), stir in gin, vermouth, bitters and violet liqueur until well chilled.
Strain into a well-chilled martini glass. Top off with claret. Express the oil
of a lemon peel by gently twisting and place along rim for garnish.

JACK THE RIPPER

★ ★ ★

THIS MODEST BUT BLUNT MARTINI IS SURE TO HEIGHTEN THE SENSES
AND MORE. WATCH OUT FOR THIS ONE, THE FLAVOR PROFILE TENDS
TO SNEAK UP ON YOU.

YIELDS 1 COCKTAIL

Ice

2 oz/60 ml dry gin (we like Bombay for this recipe)

½ oz/15 ml freshly squeezed lime juice

½ oz/15 ml almond syrup

1–2 dashes of water

1 drop lemon essential oil

Lemon peel, thinly sliced with entire pith removed for garnish

---

In a Boston shaker add 20 pieces of ice (or 1 scoop of a 16-ounce/475-milliliter
shaker), gin, lime, almond syrup and water. Shake vigorously for a count of 20,
strain and pour in a well-chilled martini glass. As you serve your guest,
drop in the lemon essential oil. Garnish with peel of lemon.

BRONX BLOOD

★ ★ ★

A SEASONALLY FRESH TAKE ON THE ORIGINAL PROHIBITION-ERA BRONX COCKTAIL THAT WAS CREATED AT THE BRASS RAIL OF THE WALDORF IN NEW YORK CITY. OUR MODERN MIX BLENDS THE JUICE OF FRESHLY SQUEEZED BLOOD ORANGES, ELIMINATING THE NEED FOR SWEET VERMOUTH, WITH SAVORY BITTERS.

YIELDS 1 COCKTAIL

---

2 oz/60 ml gin (we like Bols Genever for this recipe)

½ oz/15 ml dry vermouth (we like Noilly Prat for this recipe)

½ oz freshly squeezed blood orange juice

1 dash bitters (we like Urban Moonshine for this recipe)

Ice

1 slice of blood orange for garnish

In a bar tin, combine gin, vermouth, juice and bitters with 20 pieces of ice (or 1 scoop of a 16-ounce/475-milliliter shaker). Shake well for a count of 30. Strain into a well-chilled old-fashioned glass. Express blood orange oils by gently twisting fruit and garnish with slice.

CORPSE REVIVER NO. 2

★ ★ ★

"Four of these taken in swift succession will unrevive the corpse again."
—Harry Craddock, cocktail originator

A DRINK THAT RARELY NEEDS ANY INTRODUCTION, THE CORPSE REVIVER
NO. 2 IS AN EXCELLENT CHOICE FOR A GUEST WHO CAN HOLD THEIR OWN YET
MAY NEED A LITTLE LATE-IN-THE-EVE MORALE BOOST. DON'T UNDERESTIMATE
THIS CLASSIC BECAUSE OF ITS PERHAPS FUNNY NAME; ITS ORIGINATOR,
LEGENDARY LONDON BARTENDER HARRY CRADDOCK, KNEW EXACTLY WHAT
HE WAS UP TO WHEN CRAFTING THIS TIMELESS RECIPE. TO TRULY RAISE
A SMIRK TO THE IMBIBER'S LIPS, WE SUGGEST BUILDING WITH
BOTH ABSINTHE AND PASTIS.

YIELDS 1 COCKTAIL

---

1 oz/30 ml gin (we like Cardinal for this recipe)

¾ oz/22 ml Cocchi Americano

¾ oz/22 ml freshly squeezed lemon juice

2 dashes absinthe (we like St. George for this recipe)

1 dash pastis

1 thick lemon peel for garnish

Ice

In a Boston shaker, combine all ingredients over 20 pieces of ice (or 1 scoop of
a 16-ounce/475-milliliter shaker) and thoroughly shake for a count of 20. Strain
this opaque genius into a flute or coupe. Garnish with lemon peel.

AVIATION

★   ★   ★

A VARIATION OF THE GIN SOUR, MARASCHINO LIQUEUR IS ADDED TO
SET IT APART. TO OUR DELIGHT, CRÈME DE VIOLETTE IS BACK IN VOGUE—A
ONCE OMITTED ELEMENT FROM THE CLASSIC AS IT BECAME SCARCE IN THE
MARKETPLACE. WITH A LOVELY LIGHT-PINK HUE AND NOT TOO SWEET TASTE,
THE AVIATION WILL INSPIRE YOUR NEW LOVE OF CLASSIC COCKTAIL REVIVAL.

YIELDS 1 COCKTAIL

---

2 oz/60 ml gin (we like Green Hat for this recipe)

½ oz/15 ml maraschino liqueur (we like Luxardo for this recipe)

½ oz freshly squeezed lemon juice

½ oz/15 ml crème de violette liqueur (we like Bitter Truth Violet Liqueur
for this recipe)

Ice

1 cherry (we like Luxardo for this recipe)

In a bar tin, combine gin, maraschino liqueur, lemon juice and violet liqueur with
20 pieces of ice (or 1 scoop of a 16-ounce/475-milliliter shaker) and shake well
for a count of 30. Strain and pour into a well-chilled coupe. Garnish with
one cherry. Admire the hue and serve.

RED CLOVER

★　★　★

A MODERN EXPERIMENT ON THE FAMED FAVORITE OF THE PHILADELPHIA
MEN'S CLUB THE CLOVER CLUB COCKTAIL, THE RED CLOVER COCKTAIL TURNS
RED AND BOTANICALLY COMPLEX. FRESH RASPBERRIES ARE INSTANTLY
MARINATED WITH THE BOTANIST ISLAY DRY GIN'S COMPLEMENTARY NOTES
OF CHAMOMILE AND MINT, WHILE THE RICH FOAM BREATHES
JUNIPER SIP AFTER SIP.

YIELDS 1 COCKTAIL

---

5 raspberries

**1½ oz/45 ml dry gin (we like Bruichladdich's the Botanist Islay Dry Gin
for this recipe)**

¾ oz/22 ml fresh lemon juice

1 egg white

Ice

Bringing the complexity together is all about the foam and the reason that
a traditional preparation is imperative. In a bar tin, add fresh raspberries and
gently muddle. Combine remaining ingredients and dry shake for a count of
90. At this point, add 20 pieces of ice (or 1 scoop of a 16-ounce/475-milliliter
shaker) to chill the drink, shaking for an additional count of 10.
Strain and serve up to savor the red hue.

OLIVIA & LIMON

★ ★ ★

JUST AS AN OVER-THE-TOP BURLESQUE PERFORMANCE INCORPORATES
VARIOUS CLASSICS, SO TOO DOES THIS MARTINI. ONE TASTE OF
THIS LOOSE ELIXIR AND YOUR JUICES WILL BE FLOWING.

YIELDS 1 MARTINTI

---

2 oz/60 ml vodka

1 dash dry vermouth

1 sprig rosemary

Ice

Olive brine to taste

2 green olives

1 thinly sliced lemon wheel

Quick to make, long to savor. Pour vodka and vermouth into a Tin Play shaker,
add 20 pieces of ice (or 1 scoop of a 16-ounce/ 475-milliliter shaker) and shake
well. Strain into martini glass adding brine evenly. Garnish with olives
and lemon wheel. Enjoy a long inhale before taking the first sip.

SUMMER HEAT MARTINI

★ ★ ★

GUESTS FEELING FLUSHED? ON A HOT, HOT NIGHT OR AN AFTERNOON ON
THE VERANDA, SERVE THIS STIFF, YET COOL, MARTINI. WATERMELON, KNOWN
FOR ITS MEDICINAL USE OF REVIVING THE FAINT FROM HEAT IS
THE INSPIRATION FOR THIS COCKTAIL.

YIELDS 1 COCKTAIL

3 tsp/15 ml basil eau de vie (we like St. George for this recipe)

3 slices of cucumber

2 small wedges of watermelon for garnish

Ice

1½ oz/45 ml vodka (we like Belvedere 100 Proof for this recipe)

½ oz/15 ml gin (we like Death's Door for this recipe)

Rinse a martini glass with basil eau de vie and discard what remains. Freeze
this glass for one hour. This will be a popular drink, so freeze several prepared
glasses ahead of entertaining. In a Tin Play tin, muddle cucumber with the flesh
of one watermelon wedge. Add 20 pieces of ice (or 1 scoop of a 16-ounce/
475-milliliter shaker), vodka and gin. Shake vigorously for a count of 45, strain
and pour into your prepared basil-chilled glass. Garnish with remaining
watermelon wedge. Watch the flush fade from your guest's cheek.

MEDITERRANEAN MOJITO

★ ★ ★

THIS MOJITO IS SURE TO TOP THE OTHERS. JUST LIKE THE MERCHANTS
AND TRAVELERS FROM ANCIENT TIMES, THIS MOJITO IS RICH IN CULTURE AND
FINE IN FLAVOR. THE INGREDIENTS FUSE TOGETHER FOR A TRIP
THAT YOUR TASTE BUDS WILL NEVER FORGET.

YIELDS 1 COCKTAIL

---

5 limes for muddle and garnish

Dash of raw sugar

6 mint leaves

Ice

1½ oz/45 ml rum (we like Bacardi for this recipe)

½ oz/15 ml Campari

1 splash of soda water

½ oz/15 ml prosecco (we like Mionetto for this recipe)

Add four limes, sugar and all six mint leaves to a Tin Play shaker.
Gently guide your Tin Play 4 in 1 muddle to grind the essence of the oils from
the herbs and fruit. Add 20 pieces of ice (or 1 scoop of a 16-ounce/475-milliliter
shaker), rum, Campari and top with soda. Shake well for a count of 20. Strain
and pour into a well-chilled highball glass and top with prosecco.
Finish with a fresh lime for garnish.

RHUBARB MOJITO

★ ★ ★

IT'S TIME TO STOP AND SMELL THE RHUBARB. THIS CHOICE IS FOR THE
CONNOISSEUR OF MOJITOS. ONE TASTE AND YOU WILL BE ASKING
FOR MORE. BEST SERVED AT A SUMMERTIME BBQ.

YIELDS 1 COCKTAIL

---

1 dash Nutmeg

Zest of lime

1 tbsp/15 ml squeezed lime juice

6 leaves fresh mint

2 oz/60 ml white rum

2 oz/60 ml rhubarb syrup (see page 200)

Ice

1 oz/30 ml soda water

Sliced rhubarb

Muddle nutmeg, zest of lime, lime juice and mint. Bruise mint well. Stir in rum
and syrup, shake with 20 pieces of ice (or 1 scoop of a 16-ounce/475-milliliter
shaker). Finish with soda water and garnish with slices of rhubarb.

FOOLED YOU

★ ★ ★

THEY'VE ALWAYS WANTED TO TRY BRANDY BUT HEAR IT'S TOO STRONG.
WE'VE GOT AN ANSWER FOR THAT, A MODERN SPIN ON THE PROHIBITION-ERA
STINGER COCKTAIL. ADD A LITTLE CHOCOLATE AND THEY MIGHT BE A
BRANDY DRINKER FOR LIFE.

YIELDS 1 SMALL COCKTAIL

---

2 dashes chocolate bitters (we like Fee Brothers for this recipe)

4 sprigs chocolate mint (use regular mint in a pinch)

2 drops natural peppermint oil (we like Simply Organic for this recipe)

1½ oz/45 ml brandy (we like Rémy Martin for this recipe)

Muddle bitters, chocolate mint and peppermint oil and pour into a
cocktail glass. Then carefully pour brandy into the glass using a circular motion.
Garnish with a sprig of chocolate mint. When the scent of chocolate
hits the nostril, imbibe.

SIDECAR JOHNNY

★ ★ ★

THIS POPULAR COGNAC HAS A SMOOTH FLAVOR. THE FLAVORS OF
SWEET LEMON JUICE, ORANGE LIQUEUR AND THE KICK OF CHILI POWDER
(IF YOU CHOOSE TO USE IT) OFFSET EACH OTHER, GIVING IT A POLISHED
CONSISTENCY. A COUPLE OF THESE WILL DEFINITELY GET YOU
ON YOUR FEET AND OUT ON THE DANCE FLOOR.

YIELDS 1 COCKTAIL

---

1 tbsp/15 ml raw cane sugar for glass rimming (optional)

1 tsp chili powder for rimming (optional)

¾ oz/22 ml freshly squeezed lemon juice

½ oz/15 ml orange liqueur (we like Cointreau for this recipe)

1½ oz/45 ml cognac (we like Hennessy for this recipe)

Ice

Lemon peel for garnish

Cherries (we like Luxardo for this recipe) for garnish

If you wish to rim the glass with sugar and chili powder, now is the time. In a
shallow, flat dish, pour and sift together sugar and chili powder. Wet the outer
rim of your glass with lemon juice. Dip the outside of the rim in sugar and chili
powder, swirling twice to coat well.

In a bar tin, combine lemon juice, orange liqueur and brandy with 20 pieces of
ice (or 1 scoop of a 16-ounce/475-milliliter shaker). Shake vigorously for a count
of 20 to bring the lemon juice together with the liquors. Strain mixture carefully
into the cocktail glass, taking care to leave rimming garnish undisturbed.
Garnish with a lemon peel or marinated cherries.

SIDECAR JANEY

★ ★ ★

THIS POLITE THIRST QUENCHER WILL AMUSE YOUR TASTE BUDS IN NUMEROUS WAYS. THE ESSENCE OF OIL AND SWEET FLAVORS MIX MARVELOUSLY WITH THE ORANGE COGNAC. THE SIDECAR ORIGINATED IN PARIS IN THE 1920S AND HAS BECOME ONE OF THE MOST WELL-KNOWN DRINKS, BUT ADD A FEW VARIATIONS AND ENJOY A WHOLE NEW EXPERIENCE. CALL OVER A FEW FRIENDS AND KICK BACK WITH YOUR FAVORITE MUSIC AND ENJOY THIS RECIPE.

YIELDS 1 COCKTAIL

---

1 tsp raw sugar

1 tsp lavender flowers (set aside 5 for glass rim)

2 oz/60 ml orange-flavored brandy (we like Grand Marnier for this recipe)

½ oz/15 ml freshly squeezed lemon juice

1 tsp raw honey

1 drop neroli orange essential oil

Ice

In a mortar and pestle or dry muddling tin, combine sugar and 1 teaspoon lavender and gently crush until purple and light-brown unite. While you won't need nearly as much as you've just crushed, it will be easy to rim the glass evenly to create an aesthetic appeal. Momentarily set aside in a shallow dish. In another dish, drop in 2 teaspoons of orange brandy. Dip your glass once in the brandy dish, and then roll into the lavender-and-sugar dish to create an even rim.

To prepare this charming sidecar, in a bar tin, combine cognac, honey, juice, essential oil and 20 pieces of ice (or 1 scoop of a 16-ounce/475-milliliter shaker). Shake vigorously for a count of 30. Pour into sugar-and-lavender-rimmed glass to enjoy.

DATE NIGHT

★ ★ ★

THE LADY WANTS ANOTHER DRINK, BUT MAYBE NOT ANOTHER MARTINI. A
MODERN REVIVAL OF THE CLASSIC NIGHTCAP THE STINGER, ONCE POPULAR
AMONG THE LADIES, WE SWAP CRÈME DE MENTHE WITH FRESH PEPPERMINT
OIL. SURE TO LEAVE THE EVENING ON AN UPBEAT TONE.

YIELDS 1 SMALL COCKTAIL

---

3 oz/90 ml brandy (we like Christian Brothers for this recipe)

1 drop natural peppermint oil

Ice

Mint leaf for garnish

In a bar tin, pour brandy and peppermint oil over ice. Lightly shake for a count
of 5. Strain and pour into a glass. Garnish with mint leaf. Let the lady talk to
encourage slow enjoyment.

*1 ounce/30 milliliters of well-steeped and
chilled peppermint tea may be used when
peppermint oil is not available.*

CITRUS, SOUR & RYE

★ ★ ★

SOME GUESTS LIKE TRADITION AND WE LIKE TO CATER TO OUR GUESTS'
SENSIBILITIES. TO THE FAMILIAR CRISPNESS AND A FINISH THAT MAY STAMP
THIS COCKTAIL WITH APPROVAL, WE ADD A DASH OF ALMOND SYRUP
TO TAKE A TOUCH OFF THE BITE.

YIELDS 1 COCKTAIL

---

2 oz/60 ml rye (we like Rittenhouse Rye for this recipe)

¾ oz/22 ml freshly squeezed orange juice

3 dashes aromatic bitters (we like Fee Brothers for this recipe)

1 dash almond syrup

Ice

Maraschino cherry for garnish (optional)

Orange wedge for garnish (optional)

In a bar tin, combine rye, juice, bitters, almond syrup and 20 pieces of ice
(or 1 scoop of a 16-ounce/475-milliliter shaker). Shake vigorously for a count
of 20 and pour into a double old-fashioned glass. Garnish with cherry
and orange wedge if the guest would like.

ITALIAN OLD-FASHIONED

★ ★ ★

THE FLAVORFUL SPIN OF AN OLD-FASHIONED WILL BRING YOU BACK TO THE OLD COUNTRY. THIS UNIQUE COCKTAIL IS VERY MUCH LIKE ITALIAN CUISINE IN THE SENSE OF SIMPLICITY. FRESH INGREDIENTS AND AN ELABORATE PREPARATION MAKING ALL THE DIFFERENCE.

YIELDS 1 COCKTAIL

---

2 maraschino cherries

2 slices blood orange

4 basil leaves

2 slices red bell pepper

1 tsp/5 ml creamy honey

2 dashes bitters (we like Urban Moonshine for this recipe)

1 splash purified water

2 oz/60 ml rye (we like Hudson Manhattan for this recipe)

Ice

Chill an old-fashioned glass to build your cocktail. Muddle 1 cherry, 1 orange slice, 3 basil leaves, 1 slice of pepper, honey, bitters and water in your glass. Remove the orange rind. Add rye, 20 pieces of ice (or 1 scoop of a 16-ounce/ 475-milliliter shaker) and stir. Garnish with your remaining maraschino cherry, basil and slices of pepper and orange.

★ ★ ★

EXOTIC COCKTAILS

Herein lies a mixture of personalities, spirits and moods, which is exactly what well-concocted exotic cocktails embody. Fun to prepare, they bring together seemingly unusual ingredients that end up behaving like matches made in heaven. Flavor profiles are accentuated with flaming red wines, earthy gins, organic Proseccos, deeply steeped teas, warming brandies and floral arrangements.

This is your chance to try a whole new world of tastes and techniques. Take a risk by layering smoked herbs into your guest's glass. Please a whiskey connoisseur by washing their regular order with bacon.

We know these entertaining libations will inspire conversation and adventure on both sides of the bar.

SEA SULTAN

★ ★ ★

GUESTS ENJOYING SEAFOOD THIS EVENING, YET AREN'T SURE WHAT
TO IMBIBE? BRINY, SALTY, TANGY AND SWEET—OUR FAVORITE—A MORE
EXCITING OFFERING THAN THE OFT-SUGGESTED WHITE WINE PAIRING
SEAFOOD USUALLY RECEIVES. THIS ALSO PAIRS WELL WITH BRUNCH
AND IS WHAT WE POLITELY SERVE TO REVIVE GUESTS FROM
A LONG NIGHT OF DRINKING BEFOREHAND!

YIELDS 1 COCKTAIL

Ice

1½ oz/45 ml gin (we like Cardinal for this recipe)

½ oz/15 ml Cynar liqueur

¼ oz/7 ml lime syrup

¼ oz/7 ml pomelo or grapefruit syrup

1 pinch sea salt

2 olives for garnish

In a bar tin, combine 20 pieces of ice (or 1 scoop of a 16-ounce/475-milliliter
shaker), gin, Cynar, lime syrup and juice. Shake vigorously for a count of 45.
Pour into a well-chilled martini glass. Drop 1 pinch of salt into the center
of your cocktail and garnish with olives.

BASQUING

★ ★ ★

COMBINING SIMPLE DELIGHTS FROM BOTH THE FRENCH AND SPANISH
BASQUE REGIONS, IZARRA AND PACHARAN ARE TWO QUITE OBSCURE
BOTTLES THAT DESERVE FRONT ROW SPACING ON YOUR BAR SHELF.
SOMETIMES FORGOTTEN SPIRITS ARE THE MOST VERSATILE, AND IN THIS
CASE, YES, WE THINK SO! THE CAREFUL AND UNLIKELY HERBAL PAIRING
IS A QUINTESSENTIAL DIGESTIF THAT WILL ALLOW YOU
TO MAKE IT TO THE NEXT COURSE.

YIELDS 1 SMALL SIPPER

½ oz/15 ml yellow Izarra (almond) French Basque

1 oz/30 ml pacharan

1 cucumber for garnish

In a chilled mixing glass, combine Izarra and pacharan and stir for
60 revolutions. Into a wide-mouthed Spanish wine glass tumbler or small
jam jar, pour chilled sipper. To soak up a bit of the sugar while allowing the
medicinal properties to remain, drop in two sections of hollowed-out
cucumber. Shape into a flower or cone to create an aesthetic garnish.

THE STUFF OF LIFE

★ ★ ★

A LITTLE ELIXIR TO REMIND YOU THAT YOU'RE ALIVE . . . YOU KNOW, AFTER,
PERHAPS, YOU'VE BEEN SO LIBATIOUS IT MAY BE HARD TO TELL WHERE YOU
ARE THE NEXT MORNING! IF YOU'VE BEHAVED, YOU TOO WILL ENJOY THE
EARTHY, SATISFYING ANY-TIME-OF-DAY COCKTAIL.

YIELDS 1 COCKTAIL

Ice

2 oz/60 ml 24 karat carrot & orange juice

2 oz/60 ml Pimm's No. 1

3 chopped basil leaves

2 tsp/10 ml olive brine

1 egg white

1 dash of cayenne for garnish

In a bar tin, combine 20 pieces of ice (or 1 scoop of a 16-ounce/475-milliliter
shaker), juice, Pimm's, basil leaves, brine and egg white. Shake vigorously for a
count of 90 and pour into a chilled Collins glass. Garnish by dusting cayenne
directly in the middle of the surface of your cocktail.

THE GYPSY

AS THE NAME DESCRIBES, SO TOO DO THE INGREDIENTS. THESE WIDELY
DISPERSED COMPONENTS ARE TAKEN FROM ALL OVER EUROPE,
GIVING IT A DIVERSE TASTE. SALUD!

YIELDS 1 COCKTAIL

---

2 sprigs rosemary

1–2 dashes of bitters

1½ oz/45 ml Hendrick's Gin

½ oz/15 ml Italian bitter liqueur (we like Cynar for this recipe)

2 oz/60 ml pineapple juice

Ice

2 oz/60 ml soda water

In a Boston shaker, muddle rosemary with bitters, enjoying the earthy duo with
each press. Add gin, Cynar, juice and shake well for a count of 20. Pour over ice
and top with soda water. Add rosemary sprigs to garnish.

Very bitter, less bitter + lemon

VESPER

BOND REPLIED TO VESPER WHEN ASKED WHY HE NAMED THE DRINK AFTER HER, "BECAUSE ONCE YOU HAVE TASTED IT, YOU WON'T DRINK ANYTHING ELSE." (*CASINO ROYALE*, CHAPTER 7)

YIELDS 1 COCKTAIL

---

2 oz/60 ml gin (we like Magellan blue for this recipe)

1 oz/30 ml vodka (we like Belvedere Intense 100 Proof for this recipe)

½ oz/15 ml Cocchi Americano

Ice

1 thinly sliced lemon peel

In a Boston shaker combine gin, vodka, Cocchi Americano and 20 pieces of ice (or 1 scoop of a 16-ounce/475-milliliter shaker). Shake well for a count of 40. Strain and pour into a well-chilled martini glass and garnish with lemon peel.

The blue tint to Magellan gin is a natural result of the irises used in distilling and not of a coloring process.

PERSIMMON SOUR

★ ★ ★

WHEN IN SEASON, THE PERSIMMON YIELDS A TANGY, SWEET FLAVOR THAT GIN LOVES TO FLOW THROUGH. BECAUSE PERSIMMON IS A FIBROUS FRUIT FULL OF PECTIN, IT WILL CONTINUALLY ABSORB THE OILS OF THE ROSEMARY WITH EACH REVOLUTION OF THE ROSEMARY AS YOU STIR.

YIELDS 1 COCKTAIL

---

2 fuyu persimmons

½ oz/15 ml cardamom-clove syrup (we like Royal Rose for this recipe)

Ice

2 oz/60 ml Hendrick's Gin

1 oz/30 ml freshly squeezed Meyer lemon juice

1 Meyer lemon wedge for garnish

1 sprig of rosemary for garnish

In a Tin Play tin, muddle persimmon with cardamom-clove syrup until a thick puree remains. Muddle with love slowly so as not to bruise your fleshy fruit. Next add 20 pieces of ice (or 1 scoop of a 16-ounce/475-milliliter shaker), gin, juice and vigorously shake for a count of 45. Garnish with a slice of lemon and rosemary sprig.

MOOD MENDER

★ ★ ★

WATCH THE STRESS OF THE DAY FADE AWAY FROM YOUR GUEST'S FACE
WITH EACH SIP. MOOD-LIFTING CITRUS AND LAVENDER ARE REINFORCED
WITH GRAPPA OF ZINFANDEL. IF GRAPPA IS NEW TO YOUR GUEST, GIVE
A LITTLE HINT OF THIS ITALIAN-INSPIRED, THROAT-WARMING LIBATION!
YOU CAN DESCRIBE NOTES OF FIG, CLOVE AND CARAMEL
AS YOUR GUEST ENJOYS.

YIELDS 1 COCKTAIL

---

1 sprig of English lavender

½ oz/15 ml grappa of zinfandel eau de vie (we like St. George for this recipe)

Ice

2 oz/60 ml gin (we like St. George for this recipe)

½ oz/15 ml freshly squeezed orange juice

1 orange wheel for garnish

Pluck a ½ -inch/1-centimeter section from the bottom of your lavender sprig
and throw it into a Tin Play tin. Muddle lavender with grappa. Top this aromatic
pairing with 20 pieces of ice (or 1 scoop of a 16-ounce/475-milliliter shaker), gin
and orange juice. Shake vigorously for a count of 30, strain and pour into a
champagne flute. Garnish with a sprig of lavender and wheel of orange.

ON THE RISE

★ ★ ★

GUESTS WILL LOVE WATCHING YOU CREATE THIS CRAFT'S LAYERED LOOK
RESEMBLING A BURNT ORANGE SUNSET. AS THE NAME IMPLIES, SWEET AND
FIERY FLAVORS RISE UP THROUGH THE TOP LAYER YET ARE COOLED WITH
CRISP CARROT AND GIN. AN UNEXPECTED FINISH OF BASIL READIES
THE PALATE FOR THE NEXT SPICY SIP.

YIELDS 1 COCKTAIL

PURÉE

½ mango

2 dashes red pepper flakes

Crush mango and red pepper flakes in a mortar and pestle.

THE COCKTAIL

Ice

2 oz/60 ml Pimm's No. 1

1 oz/30 ml carrot juice

½ oz/15 ml freshly squeezed tangerine juice

1 spray chilled basil hydrosol (we like Mountain Rose for this recipe)

1 small twist of tangerine for garnish

Drizzle 2 tablespoons/10 milliliters fresh purée into a large high-stemmed
cocktail glass. In a bar tin, add 20 pieces of ice (or 1 scoop of a 16-ounce/
475-milliliter shaker) and combine Pimm's, carrot juice and tangerine juice.
Shake well for a count of 20. Strain and pour slowly over purée.
Spritz with a spray of basil and garnish with tangerine twist.

LA MARIQUITA

★ ★ ★

THIS COCKTAIL RESEMBLES THE COLORS OF A BRIGHT-RED LADYBUG, HENCE ITS PLAYFUL NAME. EACH INGREDIENT TENDS TO DANCE AND CRAWL AROUND ONE ANOTHER BASED ON ITS MOLECULAR WEIGHTS. THE MORE BITTER POMEGRANATE SEEDS WILL FLOAT WITHIN YOUR COCKTAIL, FOREVER COLLIDING WITH THE OTHER INGREDIENTS. BY THE END OF THE SIP, NOTE HOW THE POMEGRANATE SEEDS HAVE TAKEN ON A SMOKIER FLAVOR.

YIELDS 1 COCKTAIL

Ice

1½ oz/45 ml whiskey (we like Gentleman Jack for this recipe)

½ oz/15 ml red cranberry juice

1 tsp homemade rhubarb syrup (see page 200)

2 tsp/10 ml pomegranate seeds

In a bar tin, combine 20 pieces of ice (or 1 scoop of a 16-ounce/475-milliliter shaker), whiskey, juice and syrup. Shake vigorously for a count of 15, strain and pour into a cocktail glass. In your glass, add seeds and stir for 10 revolutions. Serve and suggest guest notes flavors at the first and last sip.

REVIVAL SOCIETY

★   ★   ★

OUR VERSION OF THE DISCO NAP WHEN A PILLOW SIMPLY ISN'T AVAILABLE. HERBAL, EARTHY AND SHARP, THIS DRINK IS NOTHING LESS THAN SATISFYING FOR ITS DRINKABILITY AND "HEALING" NATURE WITH THE BOTANIST, BORAGE AND CALENDULA. FLOAT A BORAGE FLOWER OR TWO TO CREATE AN OILIER MOUTHFEEL.

YIELDS 1 COCKTAIL

---

3 tsp/15 ml borage flowers, plus 2 tsp/10 ml for garnish

1 dash citrus bitters (we like Urban Moonshine for this recipe)

2 oz/60 ml dry gin (we like the Botanist Islay Dry Gin for this recipe)

¼ oz/7 ml vermouth (we like Dolin Blanc for this recipe)

Ice

1 spray calendula hydrosol (we like Mountain Rose for this recipe)

In a dry bar tin, muddle borage flowers with bitters. In your tin, combine gin, vermouth and 20 pieces of ice (or 1 scoop of a 16-ounce/475-milliliter shaker). Shake well for a count of 20 and strain into a well-chilled martini glass. Spray the surface of your libation with calendula, garnish with borage and serve.

THE STARLITE

SKIP THE APPLE PIE FOR DESSERT TO SAVOR A MORE SOPHISTICATED AFTER-DINNER COCKTAIL. YOU'LL WANT TO KEEP IT TO YOURSELF, BUT WE SUGGEST BEING NICE AND OFFERING A BITE OF YOUR APPLE SLICE TO YOUR DINNER MATE. IF DESSERT IS A MUST, THIS AROMATIC COCKTAIL PAIRS WELL WITH CARAMEL PANNA COTTA OR LIME GELATO.

YIELDS 1 COCKTAIL

Ice

2 whole star anises

Cardamom seed powder

½ oz/15 ml vanilla bitters

3 oz/90 ml apple juice

1½ oz/45 ml bourbon

1 apple slice

Pack glass with ice. The Tin Play muddling tool is perfect for the job ahead. Go to town crushing well 1 star anise. Add a dash of cardamom, bitters and apple juice to your shaker. Shake well and pour over ice. Slowly stir in bourbon while inhaling the intoxicating aromas of anise and cardamom. Garnish with slice of apple and 1 whole star anise. Sip this beauty slowly as the aromas continue to infuse with the bourbon as you drink.

WHISKEY PIG

★ ★ ★

WHISKEY WASHED WITH BACON AND FINISHED WITH VANILLA COGNAC.
IS THERE MUCH MORE TO SAY? DRAWING ON MODERN GASTRONOMIC
PLEASURES AND THE BEST MASTER MIXOLOGY HAS TO OFFER, ANY WHISKEY-
LOVING GUEST WILL SOON BE TELLING THEIR FRIENDS ABOUT THIS ONE.

YIELDS 1 COCKTAIL

---

2 oz/60 ml Whistle Pig whiskey washed with bacon (see page 205)

½ oz/15 ml Navan vanilla liqueur

1 dash black walnut bitters (we like Fee Brothers for this recipe)

1 large cube of ice

In a mixing glass stir whiskey, vanilla liqueur and bitters for
40 revolutions. Pour over 1 large cube of ice in a standard bucket
cocktail glass. Sip, very, very slowly.

DERBY DOWN

★ ★ ★

BETS ARE DOWN, THE PONIES ARE FLYING AND YOUR GUEST NEEDS
A PRESSURE DROP BEFORE THEY HIT THE FINISH LINE. QUICK TO MAKE, A
PLEASANT TASTE TO SIP AND EASY ENOUGH TO GUN DOWN WHEN THE
STAKES ARE HIGH. GARNISH WITH A MARASCHINO CHERRY—A SWEET
FINISH IS DESERVED BY ALL.

YIELDS 1 COCKTAIL

---

1 oz/30 ml bourbon whiskey (we like Woodford Reserve for this recipe)

1 oz/30 ml white rum (we like Rogue for this recipe)

½ oz/15 ml sherry (we like Dry Sack for this recipe)

¼ oz/7 ml freshly squeezed orange juice

5 cubes of ice

Maraschino cherry for garnish

In a bar tin, combine bourbon whiskey, rum, sherry and orange juice with
5 cubes of ice, shake for a count of 5 and pour into a double old-fashioned
glass over 3 medium-sized cubes of ice. Garnish with maraschino cherry.

KING'S CROSS NO. 1

★ ★ ★

WHEN WE VISIT NEW YORK CITY, WE TREK OVER TO THE BROOKLYN NAVY
YARD TO PICK UP A BOTTLE OF KING'S COUNTY MOONSHINE TO CREATE THIS
HIGH-PROOF LIBATION. SURE WE CAN GET IT SHIPPED OR GRAB IT AT
A BODEGA, BUT FOR SOME REASON THE RESULTING COCKTAIL IS ALL
THAT MORE SATISFYING AFTER HIKING FOR PROCUREMENT.

YIELDS 1 SMALL COCKTAIL

½ persimmon

2 long spears of ginger for garnish, plus one ½-in/1-cm piece for muddling

2 dashes citrus bitters (we like Urban Moonshine for this recipe)

Ice

1 splash of orange juice

3 oz/90 ml moonshine (we like King's County for this recipe)

In a Tin Play tin, muddle peeled persimmon with ginger and bitters. To your
tin, add 20 pieces of ice (or 1 scoop of a 16-ounce/475-milliliter shaker), orange
juice and moonshine. Shake vigorously for a count of 20. Strain and pour
into a highball glass and garnish with spears of ginger.

*A dramatic spirit deserves a dramatic stage.
Construct this cocktail in a thick-stemmed wine
glass with long, thick strips of pointed
ginger crisscrossing.*

KING'S CROSS NO. 2

★ ★ ★

YET ANOTHER COCKTAIL INSPIRED BY OUR FAVORITE AUTHENTIC
MOONSHINE. FOR NO. 2 WE SERVE A SWEETER VERSION. YOUR GUEST WILL
BE INTRIGUED BY MODERN-DAY MOONSHINE YET WILL STRAY BECAUSE OF
ITS BURNING REPUTATION. NOW THEY TOO CAN SAVOR A SIP, THROAT
SENSITIVITIES STILL INTACT WITH A SWEET FINISH.

YIELDS 1 COCKTAIL

---

2 oz/60 ml moonshine (we like King's County for this recipe)

2 oz/60 ml peach nectar (we like Bionaturae for this recipe)

¼ oz/7 ml pear brandy (we like Clear Creek for this recipe)

Ice

2 slices of pear for garnish

In a bar tin, combine moonshine, nectar and brandy with 20 pieces of ice
(or 1 scoop of a 16-ounce/475-milliliter shaker). Shake vigorously for a
count of 20. Strain and pour into a well-chilled cocktail glass.
Garnish with 2 slices of pear.

GINGER SNAPS

★ ★ ★

AT FIRST THE AROMAS OF AGGRESSIVE BOURBON AND SWEET CINNAMON FILL THE NOSTRILS, THEN BAM—GINGER SNAPS! WITH ONE SPRAY OF THE ATOMIZED GINGER, THE COMPLEXITY OF THIS COCKTAIL IS BORN. TO KEEP IT SNAPPY, REMEMBER TO MIST ANOTHER SPRAY ON TOP OF THIS ONE.

YIELDS 1 COCKTAIL

Ice

2 oz/60 ml bourbon (we like Buffalo Trace for this recipe)

1 oz/30 ml cinnamon foam (see tip on page 202)

1–2 sprays ginger hydrosol

Fill a tumbler about halfway with ice. Take care to slowly pour bourbon over ice. To finish, top with 1 inch of cinnamon foam and a spray or two of ginger. Sip slowly to allow the bite of the ginger and bourbon to come through the sweeter foam as it meets your mouth. Want to make ginger snap again? Pass by your patron's drink to atomize with ginger.

THE WOODSMAN

★ ★ ★

LONG, STRONG AND THE STUFF OF THE EARTH. WHILE BOTH WHISKIES
FEATURED IN THE WOODSMAN CAN CERTAINLY SPEAK FOR THEMSELVES,
THIS PAIRING OFFERS A GRASSY ARRIVAL WITH THE EXOTIC CHAI SPICES
CARRYING THE WOODIER NOTES TO THE FINISH. BEST ENJOYED WHEN
ONE HAS TIME TO SIT, SIP AND RAISE THE INTELLECT.

YIELDS 1 COCKTAIL

---

2 oz/60 ml steeped chai tea (prepared with 1 tea bag or
1 tbsp/15 ml loose-leaf chai tea)

Ice (optional)

1 oz/30 ml Compass Box Peat Monster Whisky

1 oz/30 ml Laphroaig Triple Wood Whisky

The first vital step is getting a good steep on your chai tea. Brew one tea
bag or 1 ounce/30 milliliters loose-leaf tea in 3 ounces/90 milliliters of purified
water. Allow chai to steep for ten minutes. If a tea bag has been used, press
remaining liquid into your brewing vessel. Chill tea by slowly stirring in a small
cube of ice just to take the heat off, allowing it to reach room temperature.
Once readied, pour tea into a weighted rocks glass. Premeasure whiskies,
simultaneously pouring into the chai tea. Swirl glass for a count of 5.
Allow drink to breathe for a few moments before enjoying.

*Offer ice only after a guest has taken
their first and second sips.*

THE VIG

A TWENTY-FIRST CENTURY TWIST ON THE MILLIONAIRE COCKTAIL.
WITH THIS COCKTAIL, YOU ARE THE BIG WINNER EVERY TIME: ONCE FOR
THE FLAVOR-STRIKING RINSE OF ABSINTHE AND TWICE FOR THE LONG FINISH
CREATED BY THE ABSINTHE-AGED BOURBON MARRIAGE.
ENJOY EVERY TIME.

YIELDS 1 COCKTAIL

¼ oz/7 ml absinthe, plus more for rinse

Ice

2 oz/60 ml 16 year-old bourbon (we like A. H. Hirsch for this recipe)

½ oz/15 ml orange liqueur (we like Cointreau for this recipe)

¼ oz/7 ml freshly squeezed lemon juice

2 dashes cherry juice (we like Luxardo for this recipe), plus 1 dash for garnish

½ egg white

Sparingly rinse a martini glass with absinthe, carefully pouring out the excess.
In a bar tin add 20 pieces of ice (or 1 scoop of a 16-ounce/475-milliliter shaker),
bourbon, Cointreau, lemon juice, cherry juice, the remaining absinthe and
½ egg white. For a count of 60, vigorously shake, and then strain into a martini
glass. Add 1 dash of cherry juice to center of foam and present to guest.

NICKEL DINER
AMUSE BOUCHE

★ ★ ★

THIS MINI-COCKTAIL IS INSPIRED BY THE MAGNIFICENT BACON-ENCRUSTED GLAZED DOUGHNUT THAT MADE DOWNTOWN LOS ANGELES'S NICKEL DINER FAMOUS. THE PERFECT COMPLEMENT TO FRESHLY SQUEEZED ORANGE JUICE OR MORNING COFFEE WILL DELIGHT ANY BRUNCH GOER. WARNING: GUESTS ARE LIKELY TO DEVELOP A CRUSH ON YOU AFTER SERVING!

YIELDS 4 MINI-COCKTAILS

---

6 oz/180 ml thai style coconut milk (canned) (for foam)

4 drops vanilla syrup (for foam)

4 oz/120 ml organic uncured bacon fat-washed (see page 205) bourbon (we like Maker's Mark)

4 tsp/20 ml crushed bacon for garnish

To make the cocktail, prepare a whipper with coconut milk and vanilla for at least one hour before entertaining. Presentation is everything with this one so choose four standout small clear glasses—cordials will do the trick (shot glasses are too narrow). Pour 1 ounce/30 milliliters bourbon into each glass through a strainer (to ensure steady, no-drip pouring). In a small bowl or glass, spray several thick layers of coconut-vanilla foam. With a teaspoon, layer 2 inches/5 centimeters of foam into each glass. To finish, garnish each with 1 teaspoon bacon.

L'ORANGE ROUGE BOOZY

★ ★ ★

THIS COCKTAIL IS TRULY A THING OF BEAUTY—EVERYTHING YOU EVER
WANTED IN A CRAFT COCKTAIL. KEEP AN EYE OUT FOR THIS
FIERY SNORT OF WHISKEY.

YIELDS 1 COCKTAIL

Fresh mint

3–4 slices of orange

½ cup/120 ml freshly squeezed blood orange juice

2–3 drops bitters (we like Fee Brothers for this recipe)

Ice

3 oz/90 ml bourbon (we like Bulleit for this recipe)

1 splash of soda water

Muddle mint and 3 slices of orange in a Boston shaker. Add juice,
bitters and shake well for a count of 30.

Pour into a standard bucket glass over ice. Finish this crisp refreshment
by stirring in bourbon and top with soda water. Garnish with
orange slices. Let the bourbon speak for itself.

LION'S MANE

★ ★ ★

NAMED FOR ITS RESEMBLANCE TO A LION'S THICK AND FLUFFY MANE,
THE LOOK AND TASTE IS TRUE TO ITS NAMESAKE. YOUR GUEST WILL DELIGHT
AT THEIR FIRST FROTHY SIP AS THE SAVORY FOAM SETS THE MOUTHFEEL
TO DELIVER VELVETY DRAWS OF WHISKEY.

YIELDS 1 COCKTAIL

---

1 egg white

1 tsp cane sugar

Ice

1½ oz/45 ml whiskey (we like Lion's Pride for this recipe)

1 oz/30 ml Carpano Antica vermouth

2 dashes black walnut bitters (we like Fee Brothers for this recipe)

1 tsp nutmeg for garnish

A little preparation goes a long way here. In a whipper, add egg white
and sugar, chill for an hour before use. When your whipper is nice and chilled,
combine 20 pieces of ice (or 1 scoop of a 16-ounce/475-milliliter shaker),
whiskey, Carpano Antica and bitters in a bar tin. Shake well for a count of 20,
strain and pour into a standard bucket glass. Give your whipper a grand shake,
turn upside down and at a 15-degree angle and an inch above the cocktail,
layer one thick inch of foam. A continuous, slow and circular motion yields the
most aesthetically appealing result. Shake nutmeg over foam for garnish.

EARTH ELEMENTS

★ ★ ★

AFTER A LONG EVENING OF DRINKING INTO THE WEE HOURS, SOMETIMES WE NEED TO BE BROUGHT BACK DOWN TO EARTH THE NEXT DAY. AND, SOMETIMES, OUR SENSIBILITIES SAY THIS CALLS FOR ANOTHER SOCIAL DELIGHT TO CARRY ON WITH ONE'S DAY! IF YOU'RE LOOKING TO GET STARTED WITH A LITTLE CULINARY COCKTAIL, BUT BLOODY MARY ISN'T YOUR TYPE, EARTH ELEMENTS WILL RIGHT YOUR DAY FORWARD.

YIELDS 1 COCKTAIL

3 sage leaves

2 drops tamarind syrup (we like Royal Rose for this recipe)

2 oz/60 ml pineapple juice

Ice

2 small pieces of blue cheese (we like Maytag for this recipe) for garnish

1 small roasted beet slice for garnish

2 oz/60 ml Pimm's No. 1

In a bar tin, combine sage and Tamarind syrup. Muddle these two ingredients with love as sage can become bitter when over-bruised. Next, add Pimm's No. 1, pineapple juice and ice. Shake vigorously for a count of 20 and pour into a double old-fashioned glass half full of ice. To a bar pin, slide cheese, beet and then cheese again setting over the top of your cocktail. Encourage guests to sip first and nibble later.

BLOOD & SAND

★ ★ ★

"Scotch, Scotch I love Scotch."
—Will Ferrell

WE LIKE SCOTCH SO WE BUMPED IT UP TO 1 OUNCE/30 MILLILITERS FROM
THE ORIGINAL RECIPE. CONTAINING NEITHER BLOOD NOR SAND, YOU'LL SIP,
YOU'LL WONDER WHY, BUT YOU WON'T CARE.

YIELDS 1 COCKTAIL

---

1 oz/30 ml 18-year-old Scotch whisky, or comparable
(we like Macallan for this recipe)

¾ oz/22 ml freshly squeezed orange juice

¾ oz/22 ml cherry Heering liqueur

¾ oz/22 ml sweet vermouth (we like Martini & Rossi for this recipe)

Ice

In a bar tin, combine Scotch whisky, juice, cherry Heering, vermouth and
20 pieces of ice (or 1 scoop of a 16-ounce/475-milliliter shaker). Shake well
for a count of 20, strain and pour into a chilled cocktail glass.

MILK & HONEY BUZZ

★ ★ ★

THINK CARAMELIZED PEACH PIE IN A GLASS WITH A ROYAL BUZZ
TO BOOT! IN LIEU OF DESSERT, PREPARE THIS SILKY COCKTAIL FOR GUESTS.
BRUICHLADDICH IS CHOSEN FOR ITS SIGNATURE HONEY NOTES
WITHOUT AN OVERLY SWEET OR STICKY FINISH.

YIELDS 1 COCKTAIL

---

4 oz/120 ml Thai-style coconut milk

1 tsp Pastis (we like Pernod Ricard for this recipe)

2 tsp/10 ml Y. S. Organic Farms Royal Jelly in Honey

2 oz/60 ml whiskey (we like Bruichladdich Organic Whiskey for this recipe)

½ oz/15 ml peach nectar (we like Bionaturae for this recipe)

1 whole star anise for garnish

Ice

Prepare a whipper with coconut milk, Pastis and honey for at least one hour
before crafting cocktail. In a bar tin, add 20 pieces of ice (or 1 scoop of a
16-ounce/475-millilitershaker) and combine whiskey and nectar. Shake well
for a count of 20. Strain and pour into a snifter. To finish, create a 2-inch/
5-centimeter layer of thick Pastis foam. Garnish with star anise.

BING BANG FIT

★ ★ ★

PUT SOME PEP IN YOUR GUEST'S STEP WITH THIS GREAT-FOR-MORNING COCKTAIL. AN INTERESTING ALTERNATIVE TO BOTH COFFEE AND MIMOSAS, THIS HERBAL ENLIVENING COCKTAIL DOES THE TRICK OF BOTH. EITHER SERVE SMALL COCKTAILS OR POLITELY SUGGEST GUESTS ENJOY ONE—IT'S A ZINGER!

YIELDS 1 COCKTAIL

---

2 oz/60 ml vodka (we like Belvedere 100 Proof for this recipe)

1 bag or ½-filled tea ball of yerba mate

5 muddled bing cherries

Ice

While most teas for cocktail infusing require long steeping, you'll want to be sure to do a quick steep in this case. Pour hot water over vessel with tea and steep for only two minutes. In a Tin Play bar tin, muddle bing cherries with 1 dash of vodka. Combine 20 pieces of ice (or 1 scoop of a 16-ounce/ 475-milliliter shaker), vodka and steeped tea. Shake vigorously for a count of 20, strain and pour into a champagne flute.

Utilizing the clear Tin Play shaker for a drink like this intrigues the eye and the tasting anticipation of guests as colors fade together right before serving.

SPICED THAI CRISP

★ ★ ★

THIS FIERY, SHARP COCKTAIL MIXES WELL WITH ALL THE INGREDIENTS. THE OILS FROM THE LEMONGRASS HAVE BEEN KNOWN TO ATTRACT BEES. BE CAREFUL NOT TO INGEST TOO MANY, THIS ONE IS A STINGER!

YIELDS 1 COCKTAIL

2–3 lime peels

2–3 cut lemongrass stalks

½ oz/15 ml raw honey

2 oz/60 ml vodka

1 oz/30 ml St. Germain liqueur

Ice

1–2 oz/30–60 ml soda water

1 piece candied ginger

2 lime wheels

Muddle lime peels, lemongrass and honey in a Tin Play shaker. Add vodka, St. Germain and ice. Shake vigorously for a count of 30. Pour this aromatic concoction over ice, top with soda water in a tall collins glass and garnish with candied ginger and lime wheels.

HONEY I DEW

★ ★ ★

. . . IS LIKE ONE GLOVE OF SILK AND THE OTHER OF VELVET. THIS SPICY YET COOLING INFUSION WILL BE SWEET OR SOUR DEPENDING ON THE RIPENESS OF YOUR MELON. AS DESCRIBED IN THE NAME, THIS FRESH FRUIT COCKTAIL CAN BE ENJOYED IN THE EVENING OR THE MORNING.

YIELDS 2 COCKTAILS

Ice

½ c/75 g honeydew, plus more for garnish

Fresh mint

6 oz/180 ml chili pepper–infused vodka (please see note)

5–7 dry red chili peppers

2 oz/60 ml freshly squeezed lime juice

Pack two stemless wine glasses with ice. In a dry Tin Play tin, muddle fruit and mint for one minute. Into your tin of fresh fruit and mint add 20 pieces of ice (or 1 scoop of a 16-ounce/475-milliliter shaker), vodka and lime juice. Shake well for a count of 30. Pour over ice slowly, filling glass half full to allow the honeydew to carry the spice of the chili pepper into the bowl of the glass. Garnish with fresh melon to balance the spice.

To infuse vodka, place dry red chili peppers into the vodka bottle. Store in a cool, dark area for one week before serving. Shake once every day.

MAINE ROOT FLOAT

★ ★ ★

THE ROOT BEER FLOAT GETS A CRAFTY GROWN-UP TWIST. SOME GUESTS JUST LOVE ORDERING DRINKS THAT CALL FOR WHIPPED CREAM, SO, VOILÀ, DESSERT; HAND-BLENDED WHIPPED CREAM AND WINTERGREEN–AND–ANISE-INFUSED ROOT BEER. . . . OH, DID WE SAY VODKA TOO?

YIELDS 1 COCKTAIL

---

4 oz/120 ml heavy cream for whipping

2 dashes Sambuca (one for whipped cream)

Ice

2 oz/60 ml vodka (we like Square One Organic for this recipe)

3 oz/90 ml root beer (we like Maine Root for this recipe)

1 dash chocolate bitters

1 maraschino cherry for garnish

Prepare whipped cream at least three hours ahead by mixing heavy cream with Sambuca and refrigerating. In a bar tin, pour over 20 pieces of ice (or 1 scoop of a 16-ounce/475-milliliter shaker), vodka, bitters and Sambuca. Shake vigorously for a count of 20. Strain and pour into a mason jar half filled with ice, leaving room for whipped cream. Just before adding whipped cream, pour root beer. Finish with whipped cream and a cherry.

MON CHERI
MOSCOW MULE

★ ★ ★

NOT YOUR TYPICAL SWEET MOSCOW MULE. RICH CHERRIES AND ACRID
GINGER ARE MUDDLED AND INSTANTLY INFUSED INTO THE VODKA. TOPPING
WITH THE CARBONATED GINGER BEER BRINGS A BITE TO EVERY SIP.

YIELDS 1 COCKTAIL

---

2 thin slices of ginger, plus 1 for garnish

3 cherries (we like Luxardo for this recipe), plus 1 or 2 for garnish

2 dashes aromatic bitters (we like Fee Brothers for this recipe)

2 oz/60 ml vodka (we like Tito's for this recipe)

¼ oz/7 ml freshly squeezed lime juice, plus wheel of lime for garnish

3 oz/90 ml ginger beer (we like Bundaberg for this recipe)

Ice

In a dry Tin Play shaker, muddle two slices of ginger with cherries, bitters and
vodka. You'll know you've muddled appropriately when ginger fills the nostril.
Strain and pour into a well-chilled copper mug half full of ice. Squeeze lime
juice and top with ginger beer. Garnish with a lime wheel,
cherries and ginger.

CAFFE NOIR

★ ★ ★

TENDING BAR TONIGHT? THEN YOU'LL WANT TO KNOW AT LEAST ONE SOLID ESPRESSO MARTINI. WE PROMISE THIS FLAVOR PROFILE WILL KEEP YOUR GUEST INTRIGUED WITH EACH SIP. SERVE BLACK AS MIDNIGHT.

YIELDS 1 COCKTAIL

---

2 tsp/10 ml extra-fine espresso powder

2 dashes chocolate bitters (we like Fee Brothers Aztec for this recipe)

2 drops vanilla extract

3 oz/90 ml potato vodka (we like Boyd & Blair for this recipe)

¼ oz/7 ml freshly squeezed lime juice

1 spray rosewater hydrosol (we like Mountain Rose for this recipe)

In a dry Tin Play bar tin, combine espresso powder, chocolate bitters and vanilla extract. Carefully muddle ingredients until you smell vanilla lifting from the espresso and chocolate bitters. Half fill tin with 20 pieces of ice (or 1 scoop of a 16-ounce/475-milliliter shaker) and pour in vodka and lime juice. Shake vigorously for a count of 30. Pour through a strainer into a well-chilled martini glass. When serving this noir cocktail to your guest, finish with one spray of rosewater.

PAPA DOBLE

★ ★ ★

RECEIVING ITS NAMESAKE IN HONOR OF ERNEST HEMINGWAY'S LOVE
OF STRONG COCKTAILS, THE PAPA DOBLE, AKA HEMINGWAY DAIQUIRI,
CELEBRATES A DELICIOUS OPPORTUNITY FOR MENTAL INSPIRATION. GET
GUESTS GABBING TO ENCOURAGE A LONG DRAW. RHUM CLÉMENT IS THE
RUM HEMINGWAY, HIMSELF, WOULD SELECT IF HE WERE AT OUR BAR
TODAY BECAUSE OF ITS RATHER STRONG APPEAL.

YIELDS 1 COCKTAIL

Crushed ice

1¾ oz/52 ml Rhum Clément rum

½ oz/15 ml maraschino liqueur (we like Luxardo for this recipe)

½ oz/15 ml freshly squeezed lime juice

½ oz/15 ml freshly squeezed grapefruit juice

Lime wheel for garnish

In a bar tin, combine crushed ice, rum, maraschino liqueur and juices. Shake
well for a count of 30. Strain your strong cocktail into a chilled martini glass
or coupe and garnish with lime wheel.

MATCHA HOT & SOUR

★ ★ ★

WHILE EVERYONE ELSE IS ORDERING DESSERT, SIP ON THIS. SPICY, EARTHY
AND A LITTLE SWEET, THE HOT & SOUR IS SAVORY AND ENERGETIC. WE CHOSE
A TALC-LIKE MATCHA TEA TO OFFER SEAMLESS VELVETY BLENDING.
THAI-STYLE COCONUT MILK OFFERS A CREAMY TEXTURE AND CAN
BE FOUND IN THE ETHNIC SECTION OF MOST GROCERIES.

YIELDS 1 COCKTAIL

---

4 oz/120 ml organic Thai-style coconut milk

1/2 oz/15 ml basil chili honey syrup plus 2 tsp/10 ml for whipped finish (see below)

1 teaspoon cardamom powder

2 tsp/10 ml royal matcha tea powder

2 oz/60 ml white Crusoe rum (we like One Tree for this recipe)

Ice

1 oz/30 ml freshly squeezed lime juice

1 cucumber spear for garnish

Prepare your foam ahead by combining coconut milk, 2 teaspoons/10 milliliters
honey syrup and cardamom powder in a whipper (see page 202).
Chill for at least two hours.

To make your cocktail, combine matcha powder, rum, honey and juice in
a bar tin with 20 pieces of ice (or 1 scoop of a 16-ounce/475-milliliter shaker).
Shake vigorously for a count of 20, strain and pour into a double old-fashioned
glass. Finish with a frothy layer of foam and garnish with a cucumber spear.

AU CONTRAIRE

★ ★ ★

CONTRARY TO POPULAR NOTION, NOT ALL WHISKEY IS SWARTHY. MAKING A
COMEBACK TO BAR SHELVES IS A CLEAR UNAGED RYE HINTING OF YOUNG
FLORAL NOTES THAT BALANCES WELL WITH HEARTY EVERGREEN HERBS
SUCH AS ROSEMARY. PAIR CITRUS AND APPLE TO CREATE A DEEP FLAVOR
PROFILE. BEST SERVED VERY COLD.

YIELDS 1 COCKTAIL

Ice

2 oz/60 ml white dog rye (we like Jack Daniel's for this recipe)

2 oz/60 ml freshly squeezed pink grapefruit juice

1 spray rosemary hydrosol (we like Mountain Rose for this recipe)

1 apple slice for garnish

1 sprig of rosemary for garnish

In a bar tin, add 20 pieces of ice (or 1 scoop of a 16-ounce/475-milliliter shaker),
combine rye and grapefruit juice with ice. Shake vigorously for a count of 20.
Strain and pour into a cocktail glass over ice. Spray surface of cocktail with
hydrosol and garnish with apple slice and rosemary.

*To prepare garnish, thread rosemary
through the center of apple slice.*

ROSEMARY & RYE

★ ★ ★

THIS SIMPLE BUT TASTY COCKTAIL ALLOWS YOU TO TRULY TASTE
A SNORT OF RYE WITH JUST A TOUCH OF ROSEMARY.

TASTING NOTE: BECAUSE ROSEMARY ENJOYS AN EXTENDED GROWING
SEASON OF MOIST AND DRY ELEMENTS, TRY THIS COCKTAIL AT THE BEGIN-
NING AND END OF THE SEASON. YOU'LL BE DELIGHTED AS THE CHOSEN RYE
TAKES ON A UNIQUE PROFILE AS THE SEASONS SHIFT. JOT DOWN NOTES HERE
TO REMEMBER TO SHARE TASTING DETAILS WITH GUESTS. CHOOSE YOUR
FAVORITE RYE WHISKEY IF OLD OVERHOLT IS NOT ON HAND.

YIELDS 1 COCKTAIL

**2 oz/60 ml straight rye whiskey (we like Old Overholt Straight Rye Whiskey
for this recipe)**

2 sprigs of rosemary

Ice

Muddle rye and rosemary in a Tin Play bar tin. Add 20 pieces of ice (or 1 scoop
of a 16-ounce/475-milliliter shaker), chill, strain and serve in a martini glass or
old-school coupe glass straight out of the prohibition era.

PRICKLY PEAR MEZCAL MULE

★ ★ ★

BRIGHT, SALTY AND SMOKY, THE MEZCAL MULE PAIRED WITH PRICKLY PEAR
IS AN UNEXPECTED DELIGHT. RATHER THAN MIXING THE PURÉE INTO THE
DRINK, WE ALLOW THE COARSER PARTICLES TO HOLD THE BUBBLES OF
THE GINGER BEER, ALLOWING SWEET AND SAVORY TO BLEND WITH
THE SMOKIER MEZCAL TO BE MET AT EVERY SIP.

YIELDS 1 COCKTAIL

THE PURÉE

1 prickly pear

Preparing prickly pear purée is a rewarding task. Pressing pears ahead of time
before entertaining is most ideal. If tiny hairs have not been removed, place
prickly pears in a strainer and rinse and shake under running warm water for
approximately 1 to 2 minutes. Follow with a rinse of cold water. Allow prickly
pears to drain. Peel pears, rinse again and dab dry. While a blender may help,
we love the Tin Play muddle tool and tin for this task. Add 1 pear to the tin
and press for several minutes until a slightly liquid puree remains.

THE COCKTAIL

3 tsp/15 ml fresh prickly pear purée (see above)
1½ oz/45 ml mezcal (we like Mano Negra for this recipe)
1 oz/30 ml freshly squeezed lime juice
2 dashes bitters (we like Fee Brothers for this recipe)
2 oz/60 ml ginger beer (we like Cock 'n Bull for this recipe)

In another bar tin, add your mezcal, lime juice, bitters and 20 pieces
of ice (or 1 scoop of a 16-ounce/475-milliliter shaker). Shake vigorously for a
count of 30 and pour over ice in a well-packed double old-fashioned glass.
Layer 1–2 teaspoons/5-10 milliliters of prickly pear puree to the contents over
your ice. Top with ginger beer, stir 2 revolutions and enjoy.

AJA SPICE

★　★　★

THIS SEARING SIPPER IS AN INTENSE BUT SUGARY DELIGHT. THE HOT AND
SWEET ALONG WITH THE TEQUILA BLANCO CREATE A PLEASANT BALANCE
THAT WILL KEEP YOU COMING BACK AGAIN AND AGAIN.

YIELDS 1 COCKTAIL

5–7 jalapeno slices

2 tsp/10 ml chili powder

2 slices ginger

3 oz/90 ml pineapple juice

2 oz/60 ml tequila blanco (we like 123 Organic for this recipe)

1 oz/30 ml orange liqueur (we like Combier for this recipe)

Ice

The Tin Play shaker and muddle tool are our choice to create the Aja Spice.
Add 2–4 jalapeno slices, dash of chili powder and ginger to a dry tin and
muddle gently. Once the aroma of jalapeno hits the air, add pineapple juice,
tequila and orange liqueur. Add 20 pieces of ice (or 1 scoop of a 16-ounce/
475-milliliter shaker). Shake for a count of 20 and pour into a double old-
fashioned glass. Garnish with remaining jalapeno and chili powder.

SPICE TRADE

★ ★ ★

YOU'LL BE FEELING DREAMY WITH ONLY A FEW SIPS OF PERHAPS ONE OF OUR MOST HERBAL OFFERINGS. IT'S TIME TO GET THE TORCH OUT AGAIN—THE ACTIVATION OF VOLATILE OILS IS IN THE SMOKE THIS TIME. PERFECT FOR A FOODIE OR FLAVOR CONNOISSEUR.

YIELDS 1 COCKTAIL

---

1 tsp lavender

1 chopped sprig of sage

1 dash tarragon

Ice

2.5 oz/74 ml tequila blanco

¼ oz/7 ml freshly squeezed lime juice

1 spray tulsi hydrosol (we like Mountain Rose for this recipe)

Special equipment: bell jar and pedestal stand

On a cutting board, finely chop and mix all herbs together. Place herbs to the top of your pedestal, torch until a fine white smoke appears—seconds later aromatics will fill the air, trap smoke in your bell jar.

In a bar tin, combine 20 pieces of ice (or 1 scoop of a 16-ounce/475-milliliter shaker), tequila, lime juice and a spray of tulsi. Shake vigorously for a count of 20 and pour into a double old-fashioned over one large cube of ice, saving about ½ ounce/15 milliliters to pour into a shot glass. Encourage guest to take a sip and note the flavor. Now align cocktail glass to bell jar, slide smoke over glass, pour into jar and then from bell jar back into the glass. Voilà—Spice Trade—let the new experience begin.

TRIESTE OR TREASON (AKA A MEZCAL MANHATTAN)

★ ★ ★

BUBBLE, BUBBLE TOIL AND TROUBLE COMES TO MIND HERE. MIXOLOGY IS ABOUT COCKTAILS IN THE MAKING INSPIRED BY MOMENTS IN TIME THAT COME TO SIGNIFY CLASSICS. PERHAPS THIS WOULD HAVE BEEN BETTER NAMED THE CARPE DIEM FOR ITS ON-THE-SPOT CREATION UPON A REGULAR BAR PATRON'S REQUEST FOR "SMOKE, VELVET AND, FOR THE LOVE OF GOD, NO MORE GIN."

YIELDS 1 COCKTAIL

---

2 oz/60 ml mezcal (we like Mano Negra for this recipe)

1 oz/30 ml Carpano Antica vermouth

1 large ice cube, cracked (optional)

In a mixing glass, combine mezcal and Carpano Antica. Stir for 90 revolutions. Pour into a double old-fashioned glass or over 1 large cube of cracked ice if a chilled cocktail is preferred.

LA MARIPOSA

★ ★ ★

JUST AS A BUTTERFLY TRANSFORMS, SO DOES THIS SPICY AND SWEET
TEQUILA MARTINI. AT FIRST SIP YOU TASTE SWEET, YET AS YOU GO FOR THE
NEXT A SUBTLE WARMTH MAY BE FELT ON THE CHEEK. BACK FOR THE NEXT,
NOW YOU CAN TASTE THE SPICE LIFTED UP BY THE MANGO
INTO THE RASPBERRY.

YIELDS 1 COCKTAIL

THE PURÉE

½ **mango**

3–5 drops chili oil

Preparing the purée the night before entertaining yields the best flavor
profile. To a flat dish, mash mango with a fork. Add one to three drops chili oil
(depending on desired spice level). Gently mash oil into mango, turning over
continually. Transfer to a ramekin and stir well with a spoon.
Refrigerate after preparing.

THE COCKTAIL

2 tsp/10 ml hand-blended mango chili pepper purée

Ice

2 oz/60 ml tequila blanco (we like 123 Organic for this recipe)

1 oz/30 ml agave nectar liqueur (we like Mariposa for this recipe)

¼ oz/7 ml Chambord liqueur

1 strawberry sliced in half lengthwise for garnish

In a well-chilled martini glass, drizzle purée into bottom of glass taking care
not to drip along sides. In a bar tin packed with 20 pieces of ice (or 1 scoop
of a 16-ounce/475-millilitershaker), combine tequila, agave nectar liqueur and
Chambord. Shake well for a count of 30. Through a cone sieve placed directly
over glass, slowly pour contents of tin. Garnish with strawberry slice.

PISCO SOUR

NO BAR WOULD BE COMPLETE WITHOUT THIS PERUVIAN DELIGHT. THINK OF THIS AS AN INTRODUCTION TO CLASSIC COCKTAILS FOR A GUEST WHO IS A TOUCH WARY OF EGG IN THEIR DRINK. A COCKTAIL THAT DELIGHTS ANYONE'S LIPS WILL HAVE GUESTS TRANSITIONING FROM APPREHENSIVE TO EAGERLY COUNTING IT AS THEIR NEW REGULAR.

YIELDS 1 COCKTAIL

Ice

3 oz/90 ml Macchu pisco

¾ oz/22 ml blue agave syrup

1 oz/30 ml freshly squeezed lemon juice

1 egg white

2 dashes aromatic bitters (we like Fee Brothers for this recipe)

In a bar tin, combine 20 pieces of ice (or 1 scoop of a 16-ounce/475-milliliter shaker), pisco, agave, lemon juice and egg white and shake vigorously for a count of 20. Strain and pour into a coupe and dash with bitters.

We chose Macchu because of its slightly higher proof, making it ideal for mixing with other ingredients.

CAFFE LUXE

★ ★ ★

IS IT DESSERT? A DIGESTIF? IT'S FOR THE COFFEE LOVER, BAR GOER. STAY
SHARP YET RELAXED WITH THE RICH, CREAMY INFUSION OF VANILLA AND
ANISE. REFRESH WITH A DASH OF BITTERS TO CREATE THAT LUXE EFFECT.

YIELDS 1 COCKTAIL

---

2 shots of espresso

¼ oz/7 ml Navan vanilla brandy

1 dash orange bitters (we like Fee Brothers for this recipe)

Ice

2 oz/60 ml heavy cream, chilled

¼ oz/7 ml Sambuca

In a bar tin, pour espresso, brandy, Sambuca and bitters over 20 pieces
of ice (or 1 scoop of a 16-ounce/475-milliliter shaker) and shake vigorously
for a count of 20. In a tall, slender glass, pour coffee mixture. Pour heavy cream
directly into the center of your cocktail and watch the coffee and cream
fuse to resemble marble.

WHAT A TART

★ ★ ★

NAMED FOR THE TASTE OR A GOOD STORY, YOU WONDER? WELL BOTH! WHAT A TART WAS CREATED FOR A LOVELY LADY PATRON WITH A GENTLEMAN FRIEND WHO ASKED FOR A COCKTAIL THAT WOULD MAKE HER LIPS PUCKER. SHE RETURNED TO THE BAR SEVERAL HOURS LATER WITH A DIFFERENT FELLA AND WITHOUT SKIPPING A BEAT KISSED HIM, WINKED AND SAID, "I'LL HAVE MY REGULAR." WE LIKE TO SERVE THIS COCKTAIL TO A GUEST LOOKING FOR A LITTLE SWEET MISCHIEF.

YIELDS 1 COCKTAIL

---

3 sprigs Spanish lavender, one for muddling

½ oz/15 ml Suze liqueur

Ice

¼ oz/7 ml freshly squeezed tangerine juice

2 oz/60 ml pear brandy (we like Clear Creek for this recipe)

1 thin tangerine peel for garnish

In a bar tin, add one sprig of lavender and muddle with Suze. Combine 20 pieces of ice (or 1 scoop of a 16-ounce/ 475-milliliter shaker), juice and brandy, shake for a count of 30 and strain into a well-chilled martini glass. To garnish, tie two sprigs of lavender together, floral blooms opposing one another, with a tangerine twist, and lay over the top of the glass.

RUBIES & EMERALDS

★ ★ ★

THIS DRINK IS SIMPLE TO MAKE, REQUIRES TWO TIN PLAY SHAKERS
AND WILL BE A MARRIAGE OF VIBRANT COLOR AND FLAVOR.

YIELDS 1 COCKTAIL

TIN ONE

1 oz/30 ml green Chartreuse liqueur

1 oz/30 ml fresh pineapple juice

Ice

In your Tin Play tin, combine green Chartreuse, juice and 20 pieces of ice
(or 1 scoop of a 16-ounce/475-milliliter shaker). Shake vigorously for a count of 30.

TIN TWO

3 cubes of ice

1 oz/30 ml maraschino liqueur (we like Luxardo for this recipe)

1½ oz/45 ml brandy (we like Rémy Martin for this recipe)

1 dash West Indian orange bitters (we like Fee Brothers for this recipe)

Over three cubes of ice, pour maraschino liqueur, brandy, bitters and
stir for 20 revolutions.

THE COCKTAIL

Place well-chilled martini glass at your centerline, with Tin Two held
approximately 4 inches/10 centimeters above glass and Tin One 2 inches/
5 centimeters higher. Begin pouring Tin Two to create a back-and forth-drizzle
of flaming red. One second after you begin pouring Tin Two, pour in Tin One
in a steady motion to the center of the glass. The result is reminiscent
of shiny rubies and emeralds rolling around together.

★ ★ ★

REFRESHERS

Refreshers are inviting to guests who are both new to craft cocktail culture and seasoned cocktail sippers. This is your opportunity to dive in and experiment with an array of fresh and unique ingredients that make modern craft cocktail culture so intriguing and fun. Cool gins and vodkas, bubbly sparkling wines and "life waters" (light liqueurs infused with grains and fruits) all inspire you to try your hand at infusing them with fresh sprigs of herbs and carefully chosen hydrosols. Where a deeper flavor profile is desired, we've featured rich essential oils that will instantly put a relaxed smile on a guest's face.

You'll think crisp, cool refreshment with the first few sips of these particularly reviving cocktail selections. If the night before has done your guest in, this chapter is for their morning after. These refreshers are perfectly balanced to highlight the more hydrating ingredients, so you may have to politely remind your guest that these libations do indeed contain alcohol!

CHERIMOYA BELLINI NO. 1

★ ★ ★

THE PEACH NECTAR BELLINI IS RICH—ADD A LITTLE CHERIMOYA AND IT'S
A VELVET GODDESS. STILL WITH A SILKY BOTTOM LAYER OF PEACH, WE SLIDE
IN THE FLESHY WHITE FRUIT TO THE TOP OF THE NECTAR AND MUDDLE IN
RASPBERRIES FOR A JAMMY TEXTURE. A SIMPLE INGREDIENT PROFILE
PERHAPS, YET THE BUBBLES HAVE A MIND OF THEIR OWN WHEN
THEY MEET THE TWO LAYERED FRUITS.

YIELDS 1 COCKTAIL

---

1 tbsp/15 ml organic peach nectar (we like Bionaturae for this recipe) or ¼ peach

3 raspberries

¼ cherimoya flesh, deseeded

2–3 oz/60–90 ml champagne (we like Moet & Chandon White Star for this recipe)

Orange peel for garnish

In a bar tin, combine peach nectar, raspberries and velvety cherimoya, and
gently muddle until a custard-like consistency is reached. Ladle fruit to the
bottom of a chilled champagne flute. Slowly pour champagne over fruit
until bubbles line the rim, garnish with orange peel and serve.

CHERIMOYA BELLINI NO. 2

★ ★ ★

A MORE SAVORY VERSION THAT WAS CREATED ONE AFTERNOON AT
THE REQUEST OF, "HOW ABOUT SOMETHING A LITTLE TART, PERHAPS?"
CHERIMOYA IS A VERSATILE FRUIT; ALMOST CUSTARD-LIKE, IT WILL BRING
THE FLAVOR OF WHATEVER YOU MATCH TO IT INTO ACTION. CHOOSE JUST-
RIPENED FRUIT TO OFFER THE MOST IDEAL INFUSION OF FLAVORS.

YIELDS 1 COCKTAIL

¼ cherimoya flesh, deseeded

1 tbsp/15 ml organic peach nectar (we like Bionaturae for this recipe) or ¼ peach

¼ oz/7 ml freshly squeezed orange juice

2 sprigs of thyme leaves and 1 sprig for garnish

2–3 oz/60–90 ml champagne (we like Moet & Chandon White Star for this recipe)

Miniature orange wedges for garnish

In a bar tin, muddle fruit with juice and the leaves of 2 sprigs of thyme.
Ladle mixture into the bottom of a champagne flute or divide into stemless
miniature sipping glasses and top with champagne. To finish, garnish
with orange wedges and 1 thyme sprig.

ALL THAT GLITTERS

★ ★ ★

THIS COCKTAIL HAPPENED BY ACCIDENT, THE WAY MANY CLASSICS ARE BORN, OR, RATHER, OUT OF THE NEED TO BE RESOURCEFUL TO MEET THE TASTE REQUEST OF A GUEST. WHEN AN EARLY MORNING HOUSE GUEST REQUESTED AN HERBAL YET SWEET CARBONATED CONCOCTION TO SET HIS MORNING AT EASE, ALL THAT GLITTERS WAS BORN. EASY ON THE EYES AND A.M. DIGESTION, A CLASSIC WAS BORN.

YIELDS 1 COCKTAIL

---

5 slices of cucumber

3 wedges candied ginger plus 1 for garnish

¼ oz/7 ml freshly squeezed pomelo or grapefruit juice

¼ oz/7 ml St. Germain liqueur

Ice

3 oz/90 ml champagne (we like Moet & Chandon White Star for this recipe)

In a Tin Play bar tin, combine cucumber, ginger and juice. Gently muddle until the ginger makes your nose crinkle. Add St. Germain and 20 pieces of ice (or 1 scoop of a 16-ounce/475-milliliter shaker). Shake vigorously for a count of 20, and then transfer to a well-chilled wide-bowled wine glass. Pour the champagne in a circular motion along edges of the glass and garnish with 1 wedge candied ginger. Sip the glittery infusion.

GENOVESE

THIS BASIL FROM GENOA IS THE REASON GUESTS CHOOSE TO DELIGHT
IN THIS AFTERNOON REFRESHMENT. AN EXCELLENT ACCOMPANIMENT TO
CHARCUTERIE AND GREAT ON ITS OWN, YOUR GUESTS WILL SMILE
AT THE PEPPERED BUBBLY FINISH.

YIELDS 1 COCKTAIL

---

1 tsp black pepper for glass rim dusting

1½ oz/45 ml dry vermouth (we like Martini & Rossi for this recipe)

¾ oz/22 ml freshly squeezed lime juice

4 basil leaves, 2 set aside for garnish

Ice

1 oz/30 ml Prosecco (we like Mionetto for this recipe)

Sugar cube, for garnish (optional)

Dust one edge of a double old-fashioned glass with black pepper. In a bar tin,
combine vermouth, lime juice and well-torn basil leaves. Add 20 pieces of ice
(or 1 scoop of a 16-ounce/475-milliliter shaker) and shake well for a count of 15.
Strain and pour, allowing a small amount of basil into your glass of ice.
Top with Prosecco and garnish with basil and a sugar cube (optional).

SMITHEY'S SMASH

★ ★ ★

AFFECTIONATELY NAMED AFTER A BARTENDER FRIEND OF OURS, WE ARE
ALWAYS DELIGHTED WHEN WATCHING MS. SMITHEY CAREFULLY MUDDLE HER
BERRIES, AND THEN GENEROUSLY SPLASH IN CHAMPAGNE OVER THE FRUIT.
WE'VE COMPLEMENTED THE CREATION WITH A FINISH
OF TANGY CHERRY AIR.

YIELDS 1 COCKTAIL

---

2 oz/60 ml cherry liqueur (we like Luxardo for this recipe)

1 oz/30 ml cranberry juice

Ice

5 blackberries

2 oz/60 ml vodka (we like Death's Door or Belvedere 100 Proof for this recipe)

¼ oz/7 ml St. Germain liqueur

½ oz/15 ml Prosecco (we like Mionetto for this recipe)

In a Tin Play tin, pour cherry liqueur and cranberry juice over 1 ice cube
and shake vigorously for a count of 30. In another Tin Play tin, muddle blackberries and combine vodka and St. Germain. Shake vigorously for a count of
20. In a well-chilled fluted glass, pour over ice and top with Prosecco. To create
an airy allure, shake your cherry and cranberry tin for yet another count of 30,
strain and slowly pour over the top of the Prosecco to meet the bubbles,
finishing with a fuchsia hue.

MOROCCAN AFTERNOON

★ ★ ★

THIS MIDDLE EASTERN, SUPER FOOD–INSPIRED SPIRIT, ALSO KNOWN AS AN INDIAN APPLE, IS SURE TO PLEASE THE PICKIEST OF DRINKERS. THE INFUSED POMEGRANATE VODKA BLENDS SEAMLESSLY WITH THE FRESH JUICES TO COMPOSE A PUT-THE-ROUGE-ON-YOUR-CHEEK, MID-AFTERNOON DELIGHT.

YIELDS 1 COCKTAIL

THE CARDAMOM–INFUSED HONEY

3 cardamom pods or 1 tsp powdered cardamom

3 oz/90 ml organic raw honey

Preparing cardamom infused honey is a sensual delight. In a mortar, crush 3 cardamom pods until both large and fine pieces remain. Set aside large pieces and use fine pieces. In a glass bowl or jar, mix cardamom with honey. While crushing cardamom will yield the freshest, most aromatic result, powdered cardamom will do in a pinch.

THE COCKTAIL

2 oz/60 ml pomegranate vodka (we like Van Gogh for this recipe)

2 oz/60 ml freshly squeezed grapefruit juice

Ice

1 oz/30 ml cardamom-infused honey

1–2 oz/30–60 ml soda water

Wedges of grapefruit for garnish

In a shaker, add vodka, juice and 20 pieces of ice (or 1 scoop of a 16-ounce/475-milliliter shaker). Shake well for 90 counts until tin is very cold. Strain and pour into a standard bucket glass. Stir in cardamom honey. Stir slowly for 30 counts or until you see the ribbons of honey melt away into the drink. Top with soda water and garnish with grapefruit.

ELDERFLOWER SIPPER

★ ★ ★

WHILE VODKA IS STILL HAVING A HARD TIME FINDING ITS WAY INTO CRAFT COCKTAIL CULTURE, IT COULD NOT FIT ANY MORE PERFECTLY HERE WITH THIS AROMATIC, PLAYFUL AND ROMANTIC SIPPER. LOVELY FOR AN AFTERNOON ON THE VERANDA OR TO WARM A CHILLY MOOD, THE INFUSION OF LAVENDER AND ROSE WILL MELT AWAY ANY THOUGHTS OF THE DAY.

YIELDS 1 COCKTAIL

Ice

2 oz/60 ml vodka (we like Square One Organic for this recipe)

3 oz/90 ml lemonade (fresh pressed, preferred)

1½ oz/45 ml elderflower liqueur (we like St. Germain for this recipe)

1 oz/30 ml lavender syrup

1 spray rosewater hydrosol (we like Mountain Rose for this recipe)

In a bar tin with 20 pieces of ice (or 1 scoop of a 16-ounce/475-milliliter shaker), gently stir vodka, lemonade, elderflower liqueur and lavender syrup for a count of 30. Pour over ice in a glass with a bowl such as a stemless wine glass. Spray rose water over ice and stir into ice 3 revolutions.

BREAK OF DAWN

★ ★ ★

A LEMONADE COOLER WITH YOUR BEST INTERESTS IN MIND. A PERFECT
ACCOMPANIMENT TO BRUNCH THAT WILL ASTRINGE THE SOUL OF THE BEST
OF 'EM. THE VELVET FALERNUM COMBINES A STRIKING PROFILE OF SWEET,
VANILLA AND CLOVE LAYERED INTO A PEPPERY PUNCH
OF GINGER AND LAVENDER.

YIELDS 1 COCKTAIL

Ice

2½ oz/74 ml peppered vodka (we like Stolichnaya for this recipe)

¼ oz/7 ml Velvet Falernum liqueur

1 tsp lavender-lemon syrup (we like Royal Rose for this recipe)

In a Boston shaker, combine 20 pieces of ice (or 1 scoop of a 16-ounce/
475-milliliter shaker), vodka, liqueur and syrup. Shake vigorously for a count
of 20 and pour into a highball glass packed with ice.

THYME, LIME & LAVENDER CRISP

★ ★ ★

A COOL, CRISP AND SAVORY REFRESHMENT THAT WILL PLEASE THE PALATE OF ALL GUESTS ON A HOT SUMMER DAY. AKIN TO LAVENDER LEMONADE, THIS FLORAL ARRANGEMENT IS BOTH A MENTAL SOOTHER AND A THIRST QUENCHER. THE FIRST ONE GOES DOWN FAST; BE SURE TO SAVOR THE SECOND SLOWLY TO TAKE IN THE BOUQUET OF FLAVORS.

YIELDS 6 SMALL COCKTAILS

Ice

6 sprigs lavender, 3 for garnish

6 sprigs thyme, 3 for garnish

1 oz/30 ml freshly squeezed lime juice

3 oz/90 ml St. Germain liqueur

12 oz/350 ml vodka

1 splash of soda water

Pack 6 glasses half full with ice. Muddle 3 sprigs each of lavender and thyme with lime juice in a bar tin. Add St. Germain and vodka to shaker. Shake well for a count of 30 and pour over ice. Top each with soda water. Garnish the top of each glass with lavender and thyme. Encourage guests to stir in lavender and thyme garnish as they sip.

IT'S NOT A MIRAGE

★ ★ ★

BEST SERVED IN THE SUMMER OR WHEN A BIT OF REVIVING IS IN ORDER. THIS
COOL, SOOTHING SWATH OF FLAVOR COLLECTS THE SUCCULENT FIBERS
OF BOTH AGAVE AND ALOE AND BRINGS THEM TOGETHER WITH THAI BASIL.
PAIRS WELL WITH SUSHI AND KNOWS HOW TO HOLD ITS OWN.

YIELDS 1 COCKTAIL

---

1 tsp blue agave syrup

1 in/2 ½ cm fresh aloe vera cut into a spear or ¼ oz/7 ml aloe vera juice

3 leaves Thai basil plus 1 for garnish

3 slices cucumber

2 oz/60 ml gin (we like Cardinal for this recipe)

Ice

1 oz/30 ml soda water

In a bar tin, muddle agave, aloe, basil and cucumber. Combine gin and
shake well for a count of 30. Strain and pour over a tumbler full of ice,
top with soda and garnish with Thai basil.

FLOWER BOMB

★ ★ ★

CELEBRATE THE FIRST SIGNS OF SPRING WITH THIS SEASONAL
COCKTAIL BEAMING WITH COLOR AND OVERFLOWING WITH FLORAL TONES
THROUGHOUT. CRISP GIN OPENS THE SENSES; BEFORE YOU KNOW IT,
YOU'LL BE NOTICING MORE THAN JUST THE FLOWERS.

YIELDS 1 COCKTAIL

---

2 oz/60 ml gin (we like Hendrick's for this recipe)

¼ oz/7 ml violet liqueur (we like Bitter Truth for this recipe)

1 drop neroli orange essential oil

1 spray calendula hydrosol (we like Mountain Rose for this recipe)

1 egg white

Ice

In a Tin Play bar tin, combine gin, violet, essential oil, calendula and
egg over 20 pieces of ice (or 1 scoop of a 16-ounce/475-milliliter shaker)
and shake vigorously for a count of 30. In a well-chilled coupe
or martini glass strain and pour.

*Use the clear tin to show guests how
the color composition develops as you shake.*

SIPPER SENSUAL

★ ★ ★

THE PERFECT BLIND DATE OR DAYDREAMING SIPPER. EXOTIC YLANG-YLANG ESSENTIAL OIL RUSHES TO ALL CORNERS OF THIS LITTLE GEM AS IT'S STIRRED THROUGH AND THROUGH. IF YOUR DATE SEEMS LIKE THEY'RE NOT LISTENING, DON'T BE OFFENDED, THEY'RE JUST TAKING IT ALL IN.

YIELDS 1 SMALL COCKTAIL

---

1 Meyer lemon

2 oz/60 ml gin (we like Sipsmith for this recipe)

1 long sprig of thyme

1 drop ylang-ylang essential oil

Ice

Preparing your lemon-thyme-infused garnish is an essential first. Roll one small Meyer lemon on the bar top or counter to assist in expressing juices within. Taking care not to lose the juice, slice over a shallow bowl. To each half divide the sprig of thyme and carefully muddle into the lemon flesh. In a mason jar, squeeze the juice of one half with fragments of thyme. In a bar tin, combine 20 pieces of ice (or 1 scoop of a 16-ounce/ 475-milliliter shaker), the other half of lemon, gin and ylang-ylang. Shake vigorously for a count of 30 and pour over lemon in jar. Breathe slowly and enjoy.

BLOOD ORANGE FRENCH 75

★ ★ ★

WITH INGREDIENTS BEARING A RESEMBLANCE TO THE POWERFUL KICK OF A
FRENCH 75 MM FIELD GUN, THIS DRINK WAS CREATED IN PARIS AND BROUGHT
TO NEW YORK IN THE 1930S. THIS COCKTAIL WOULD BE AN EXCITING
ALTERNATIVE TO THE MIMOSA.

YIELDS 2 COCKTAILS

---

4 oz/120 ml gin (we like Nolet's for this recipe)

3 oz/90 ml freshly squeezed lemon juice

1 oz/30 ml freshly squeezed blood orange juice

Ice

1 oz/30 ml chilled champagne

Blood orange twists for garnish

In a bar tin add gin, juices and 20 pieces of ice (or 1 scoop of a 16-ounce/
475-milliliter shaker). Shake with vigor. To demonstrate its namesake, pour
dramatically into a collins glass and top with champagne.
Garnish with blood orange peels.

FERNET ME NOT

★ ★ ★

DON'T LET GUESTS BE FOOLED BY THE SIMPLE LOOK—AS SOON AS THE
AROMATICS OF THIS HERBAL COCKTAIL HIT THE AIR, IMBIBERS ARE IN FOR A
TREAT. THE SECRET IS IN THE OVERNIGHT SOAKING OF YOUR ORANGE TWIST
IN FERNET-BRANCA. A COCKTAIL SOON TO BE REMEMBERED BY THE SENSES
AND THE PALATE, BUT PERHAPS NOT THE NEXT MORNING?

YIELDS 1 COCKTAIL

---

1 orange twist

2 oz/60 ml Fernet-Branca

1 oz/30 ml gin (we like Bombay Sapphire for this recipe)

½ oz/15 ml Lillet Blanc

1 tsp Combier Liqueur d'Orange

Ice

Cut a thick orange twist long enough to wind from the bottom to the top of
a standard champagne flute. In a glass container, place twist and generously
cover in Fernet-Branca. Store overnight.

In a bar tin, combine gin, Lillet and Combier with 20 pieces of ice (or 1 scoop
of a 16-ounce/475-milliliter shaker) and shake vigorously for a count of 30.
Strain and pour into a champagne flute. Just before serving guest, place
Fernet-Branca–soaked twist carefully into the center of the cocktail. Watch
the expression on your guest's face as they take in the eye-opening scent.

FRAMBOISE SERIEUX
★ ★ ★

THIS ALMOST FREEZING RASPBERRY COCKTAIL MAKES A STUNNING PRESENTATION AT ANY BAR. FOR THE GUEST ASKING FOR THE COMBINATIONS OF COOL, CRISP AND TART, THIS AFTER-DINNER COCKTAIL WILL KEEP OTHER HEADS TURNING. A TRUE PALATE-CLEANSING EXPERIENCE.

YIELDS 1 COCKTAIL

½ oz/15 ml raspberry eau de vie plus 1 tsp to rinse glass (we like St. George)

½ oz/15 ml fresh raspberries

¼ oz/7 ml freshly squeezed lemon juice

Ice

2 oz/60 ml dry gin (we like St. George for this recipe)

3 small twists of lemon for garnish

Rinse a martini glass with 1 teaspoon eau de vie and discard. Eau de vie is thick; take care not to drip along the outside edges when rinsing. Chill this glass for at least one hour before serving. In a Tin Play tin, add raspberries, lemon juice and ½ ounce/15 milliliters eau de vie, and muddle gently until raspberries are completely pureed. Set aside momentarily in your freezer. In a clean tin, add 20 pieces of ice (or 1 scoop of a 16-ounce/475-milliliter shaker) and gin and shake vigorously until a thin skin of ice appears on your shaker. Ice-cold gin is of utmost importance. Strain and pour gin into the shaker of raspberries, shake well for a count of 20 and pour into a martini glass. Finish by expressing the oils of three lemon twists and garnish.

ROSE'S BLUSH

★ ★ ★

AN ELEGANT, STRIKING SIPPER THAT WILL GET YOUR GUESTS SITTING UP STRAIGHT. WITH ESSENCES OF GRAPEFRUIT, ROSE AND JUNIPER, A RATHER MIND-CLEARING, ATTENTION-GETTING SPIRIT WILL BE EVOKED. ALWAYS SERVE COLD AND CRISP.

YIELDS 1 COCKTAIL

---

1 slice fresh-cut radish

2 oz/60 ml gin

Ice

1 oz/30 ml freshly squeezed grapefruit juice

¼ oz/7 ml Amer Picon liqueur

2 oz/60 ml rosé wine, chilled

½ oz/15 ml soda water

Rose petals for garnish

In a Tin Play shaker, gently muddle slice of radish with gin. Combine 20 pieces of ice (or 1 scoop of a 16-ounce/475-milliliter shaker), gin, grapefruit juice and Amer Picon to tin and shake vigorously for a count of 30. Strain and pour into a well-chilled cocktail glass. Retrieve chilled rosé, pour into the center of your cocktail and top with a spritz or two of soda water. Float rose petals for an aesthetic appeal.

THISTLE & ROOT

★ ★ ★

ONE OF OUR FAVORITE AFTER-DINNER DRINKS. SIMPLE TO PREPARE, EARTHY AND AN IDEAL PALATE CLEANSER TO, AHEM, MOVE ON TO MORE SERIOUS DRINKING. WE CHOSE THE TERROIR FOR IT IS REMINISCENT OF DOUGLAS FIR AND COASTAL CALIFORNIA SAGE. IF GINSENG ROOT IS OBSCURE IN YOUR LOCALE, BAGGED GINSENG TEA CAN BE STEEPED.

YIELDS 1 SMALL COCKTAIL

---

1 oz/30 ml Cynar liqueur

2 oz/60 ml St. George Terroir Gin

Ice

3 tsp/15 ml ginseng root elixir

In a Boston shaker, combine Cynar, gin and 20 pieces of ice (or 1 scoop of a 16-ounce/475-milliliter shaker). Shake well for a count of 20. Strain and pour into a small, stemmed cocktail glass and add ginseng elixer to the top of your cocktail to finish.

THE TASTE OF COOL

★ ★ ★

IF CRISP WERE A FLAVOR, THAT'S WHAT WE'D SAY IS EMBODIED IN
THE TASTE OF COOL. THE SECRET TO DEFINING THIS TASTE IS IN THE
MUDDLING OF CUCUMBER WITH LEMON VERBENA. THE MUDDLED
CUCUMBER OFFERS HENDRICK'S GIN THE OPPORTUNITY
TO MARRY, LIFTING THE HERBAL NOTES.

YIELDS 1 COCKTAIL

---

2 rounds of sliced cucumber

2 sprays lemon verbena hydrosol (we like Mountain Rose Organic for this recipe)

Ice

3 oz/90 ml Hendrick's Gin

¼ oz/7 ml soda water

1 thinly sliced cucumber skin

Muddle 1 round of cucumber with 1 spray lemon verbena. In a bar tin,
add 20 pieces of ice (or 1 scoop of a 16-ounce/475-milliliter shaker), gin and
soda water. Shake vigorously for a count of 20 and pour in glass with ice. Top
with an additional spray of lemon verbena. Garnish with slice and round of
cucumber. Suggest guest nibble the garnish that has lifted the
herbal elements of the Hendrick's.

SUBDUED

THIS SOFT BUT LUSTROUS MARTINI IS A FAVORITE IN THE CRAFT COCKTAIL COMMUNITY. WATCH YOUR MARTINI BLOSSOM WITH THE ESSENCE OF ELDERFLOWER AND FRESH LEMON.

YIELDS 1 COCKTAIL

1½ oz gin (we like Tanqueray 10 for this recipe)

¼ oz/7 ml freshly squeezed lemon juice

½ oz/15 ml St. Germain liqueur

1 dropper rhubarb syrup (see page 200)

Ice

In a bar tin add gin, juice, St. Germain, rhubarb syrup and 20 pieces of ice (or 1 scoop of a 16-ounce/475-milliliter shaker). Shake vigorously until a skin of ice appears on your shaker. In a chilled martini or double old fashion glass, strain and pour.

CARTE BLANCHE

★ ★ ★

THIS LIGHT-BODIED COCKTAIL ALLUDES TO THE FAMOUS JAMES BOND.
YOU KNOW, HE WASN'T ALWAYS SIPPING FROM A STEMMED GLASS. IT SHOULD
BE ENJOYED IN A RELAXING SETTING AS JAMES WOULD IN HIS FLAT.
IN THIS CASE, WE STIR.

YIELDS 1 COCKTAIL

---

2 oz/60 ml bourbon (we like Basil Hayden's for this recipe)

3 dashes cherry bitters

Ice

1 whiskey-marinated cherry for garnish

3 small lemon twists for garnish

In a bar tin combine bourbon, bitters and 20 pieces of ice (or 1 scoop
of a 16-ounce/475-milliliter shaker). Stir and strain into standard bucket glass
over ice. Garnish with marinated cherries and lemon twists.

SAFFRON PLUM SOUR

★ ★ ★

AN UNLIKELY COMBINATION OF HERBS, CITRUS AND ROOTS THAT GETS THE
JUICES FLOWING—A SAVORY DIGESTIF BEST SERVED AFTER A HEARTY MEAL.
AS IF THE TRADITIONAL PLUM SOUR WASN'T GOOD ENOUGH ON ITS OWN, WE
INFUSE EXOTIC AND PUNGENT SAFFRON INTO THE PLUM TO RELEASE THE
BITE OF BOURBON RIGHT INTO THE GUEST'S MOUTH. FINISH WITH A SLICE
OF TURNIP TO OFFER AN EARTHY PALATE CLEANSER.

YIELDS 1 COCKTAIL

½ **plum**

1 oz/30 ml saffron syrup (we like Royal Rose for this recipe)

Ice

2 oz/60 ml bourbon (we like Baker's for this recipe)

2 oz/60 ml freshly squeezed lemon juice

1 oz/30 ml purified water

1 tsp raw honey

1 slice yellow turnip for garnish

In a Tin Play shaker, muddle plum and syrup together until a slight pungent
odor fills your senses. To this muddled mixture add 20 pieces of ice (or 1 scoop
of a 16-ounce/475-milliliter shaker), bourbon, lemon juice, water and honey.
Shake vigorously for a count of 20 and pour over a double old-fashioned
glass packed with ice. Garnish with a slice of turnip and
encourage palate-cleansing nibbles.

HIGH TEA

★ ★ ★

. . . BECAUSE IT WILL GET YOU HIGH. THAT IS, THE SPECIAL COMPASS BOX FLAMING HEART SCOTCH WHISKY WILL HEIGHTEN AND WARM YOUR GUEST'S SENSES. THE PERMEABLE NATURE OF GREEN TEA LEAVES RAISES UP THE CITRUS AND HERBAL CORIANDER THAT WE LOVE SO MUCH ABOUT FLAMING HEART.

YIELDS 1 COCKTAIL

---

2 tsp/10 ml loose green tea leaves
2 oz/60 ml Compass Box Flaming Heart Scotch whisky

Add ingredients to a mixing glass and stir for 90 revolutions. No need to steep the tea as stirring will bring out just the right amount of flavor. Strain and pour into a double old-fashioned glass.

TEQUILA BLANCO RICKEY

★ ★ ★

AS CRISP AS A GIN RICKEY BUT WITH THE ELEMENTS OF BUBBLY CITRUS,
THE TEQUILA BLANCO RICKEY IS A HOT-DAY FAVORITE. BEST SERVED
POOLSIDE WITH SOME COOL FRIENDS.

YIELDS 1 COCKTAIL

1½ oz/45 ml tequila uno blanco (we like 123 Organic for this recipe)

¼ oz/7 ml blue agave nectar

¾ oz/22 ml fresh lime juice

Ice

1 oz/30 ml soda water

Lime zest for garnish

Salt for rimming (optional)

Combine tequila, agave and lime juice in a Boston shaker with 20 pieces
of ice (or 1 scoop of a 16-ounce/475-milliliter shaker) until a thin icy skin appears
on your tin. Pour and strain over 1 large ice cube in a standard bucket glass and
top with soda. Garnish with zest of lime peel. Like a bite? Balance the drink
with a thin rim of salt.

★   ★   ★

PARTIES & PUNCHES

Ever noticed how a spiked punch can spark the life into a party? Parties and punches are opportunities to introduce both taste and creativity to any bar or gathering, taking the craft cocktail experience to a communal level.

This collection of cocktails invites guests to drink like they eat, calling on ingredients from the kitchen. A few of these libations are the answer to pleasing your sweet tooth while others are savory and herbaceous.

We have taken care to suggest small sippers and sometimes mini-cocktails so that you may enjoy not one, but two of these playful libations. We encourage guests to do tasting flights of punches with friends or among strangers to break the ice. We hope these entertaining libations will inspire conversation and adventure on both sides of the bar.

MÉNAGE À TROIS

★ ★ ★

A LITTLE GAME OF FLAIR SOMETIMES GOES A LONG WAY. A TRIO OF THREE PLAYFUL COCKTAILS MEANT TO BE CREATED FOR A GROUP OF THREE GUESTS EXHIBITING ADVENTUROUS SPIRITS! TWO ARE ALIKE WITH THE THIRD AN ALLURING CONTRAST. ENCOURAGE GUESTS TO SIP AND SHARE AMONG THEMSELVES. IF GUESTS SEEM TO ENJOY PLAYING ALONG, PLACE THREE SMALL COCKTAIL GLASSES BEFORE THEM. ADD ALL THREE REMAINING DRINKS BACK INTO A SHAKER SANS ICE, STRAIN AND POUR INTO THREE GLASSES. THE NEW FLAVOR PROFILE SIGNIFIES AN UNEXPECTED UNION OF FLAVORS.

NOTE: THIS INVOLVES CONSTRUCTING THREE SEPARATE COCKTAILS, TWO OF WHICH ARE SIMILAR.

THE ALLURING CONTRAST

YIELDS 1 COCKTAIL

3 slices red pepper

2 wedges of lime

2 oz/60 ml mezcal (we like Vida for this recipe)

2 oz/60 ml freshly squeezed orange juice

Ice

2 strips beef jerky

In a Tin Play tin, muddle slices of red pepper and wedges of lime. In your shaker, combine mezcal, orange juice and 20 pieces of ice (or 1 scoop of a 16-ounce/475-milliliter shaker). Shake lightly for a count of 15. Strain and pour into a double old-fashioned glass. Garnish with jerky.

ALIKE NO. 1

3 oz/90 ml passion fruit liqueur (we like Passoã for this recipe)

2 oz/60 ml fresh pineapple juice

4 leaves of basil, 2 for garnish

1 passion fruit for passion fruit "caviar" garnish

In a Tin Play tin, combine liqueur, pineapple juice, torn basil and 20 pieces of ice (or 1 scoop of a 16-ounce/475-milliliter shaker). Shake lightly, strain and pour over a double old-fashioned full of ice. Garnish by scooping passion fruit seeds with a teaspoon and delicately placing on a basil leaf you've just placed on the surface of your cocktail.

ALIKE NO. 2

YIELDS 1 COCKTAIL

2 oz/60 ml Rémy Martin Cognac

¼ oz/7 ml red cranberry juice

1 dash aromatic bitters

3 tsp/15 ml pomegranate seeds for garnish

1 large cube of ice

In a chilled mixing glass, combine Rémy, juice and bitters. Stir for 20 revolutions. Pour over a glass containing one large ice cube and garnish with floating pomegranate seeds.

VIOLET'S PARTY

★ ★ ★

THANKS TO THE REVIVAL OF CRÈME DE VIOLETTE, THIS CREATION IS A LITTLE SIPPER FROM HEAVEN—MEXICAN HEAVEN, THAT IS. INSPIRED TO BRING FLORAL NOTES TO SOMETHING OTHER THAN GIN AND BRANDY, WE KNOW GUESTS WILL LOVE THIS TEQUILA REPOSADO SPECIAL. A LIBATION SURE TO SIGNAL THE COMMENCEMENT OF CONVERSATION IN ANY GROUP OF STRANGERS.

YIELDS 2 COCKTAILS

---

3 oz/90 ml reposado (we like 123 Organic for this recipe)

1½ oz/45 ml crème de violette (we like Bitter Truth for this recipe)

½ oz/15 ml freshly squeezed lime juice

Ice

1 lime wedge for garnish

In a bar tin, combine reposado, crème de violette and juice. Shake well for a count of 30 and pour over ice into a standard bucket glass. Garnish with lime.

123 Organic Reposado was created as a sipping tequila. As guests begin chatting, offer an extra taste of this special reposado on its own to teach them how flavor profiles may be born into craft cocktails.

EXPRESS RUSH

★ ★ ★

AN UNEXPECTED FLAVOR COMBINATION THAT CREATES AN EXHILARATING
RUSH WHEN SIPPED DURING THE FINAL COURSE OF THE PARTY. TANNIC,
SWEET AND SAVORY, THIS CREAMY, CHILLED DELIGHT CAN BE SERVED IN LIEU
OF DESSERT. AN EXCELLENT FINISH TO LAMB OR BEEF ROAST.

YIELDS 1 COCKTAIL

---

1 freshly squeezed wedge of blood orange

Ice

1 scoop lime sorbet

1 oz/30 ml limoncello liqueur

2 oz/60 ml cabernet sauvignon (we like Zero Defects for this recipe)

1 thin wedge of blood orange for garnish

3-5 blackberries for garnish

Squeeze orange into the bottom of a large, wide-mouth red wine glass and
rinse. Discard any excess juice. Freeze this glass well. Once glass is frozen, add
20 pieces of ice (or 1 scoop of a 16-ounce/475-milliliter shaker) and 1 standard
ice cream scoop of lime sorbet into the frozen glass. Pour limoncello over
sorbet and top with wine. Garnish with orange wedge and blackberries.
Watch for the rush on your guest's face.

SANGRIA MANZANA

★ ★ ★

YOU KNOW THOSE FALL DAYS WHEN IT HEATS UP OUT OF NOWHERE AND
EVERYONE IS OUT DINING ON THE VERANDA? SANGRIA MANZANA IS OUR
SEASONAL FAVORITE TO PROVIDE SAVORY REFRESHMENT ON THOSE DAYS.
SERVE WITH GREEN APPLES FOR A TANGIER PUNCH AND RED FOR SWEETER.

YIELDS 6–8 COCKTAILS

---

10 crushed Marcona almonds

3 green apples

1 cinnamon stick zested, more sticks for garnish (optional)

1 orange, zested and juiced

2 oz/60 ml orange liqueur (we like Cointreau for this recipe)

1 lime sliced into wheels

1 750-ml bottle Organic Wine Company's Sol de Agosto Tinto

3 tsp/15 ml raw honey

Ice

8 oz/240 ml soda water

You'll want to crush your almonds and core and chop two of your apples
before getting to the punch. A Tin Play 4 in 1 muddle or large mortar and pestle
are ideal for the almonds. Crush almonds as finely as possible and pour into a
large pitcher. Then add apples, cinnamon, orange zest and juice, Cointreau, lime
wheels and wine. Stir for 50 revolutions, add honey and stir for an additional
10 revolutions. Add 30–40 pieces of ice (or 1½-2 scoops of a 16-ounce/
475-milliliter shaker) to cool sangria.

To serve, half fill a large wine glass with ice and pour Sangria Manzana over it.
Slice last apple and garnish each drink with one slice and a cinnamon stick.
Top each glass with approximately 1 ounce/30 milliliters of soda water.

ZANZIBAR PUNCH

★ ★ ★

THIS COLORFUL AND EXTRAVAGANT PUNCH IS SURE TO BE THE "LIFE OF
THE PARTY." ITS NUMEROUS INGREDIENTS MIXED TOGETHER OVER TIME YIELD
A DANGEROUS BUT DELIGHTFUL FUSION. TAKE CAUTION; IF THE FRUIT IS
INGESTED YOU MIGHT FIND YOURSELF THREE SHEETS TO THE WIND
OF ZANZIBAR.

YIELDS 10–12 COCKTAILS

---

1 750-ml bottle cabernet sauvignon, chilled

16 oz/473 ml aged rum, chilled

12 oz/350 ml freshly squeezed lemon juice (from about 8 medium lemons), chilled

6 oz/177 ml sweet syrup or 4 oz/120 ml organic creamy honey

3 oz/90 ml yellow Chartreuse liqueur

1 oz/30 ml orange-flavored brandy (we like Grand Marnier for this recipe)

6 dashes blood orange bitters

1 dropper neroli orange essential oil

Ice

Wedges of blood orange cut for garnish

Place all ingredients in a large punch bowl or container. Add your ice
and wedges, and serve chilled. We suggest allowing it to sit
for 24 hours for best results.

BOARDWALK PUNCH

★ ★ ★

THIS SUMMERTIME DELIGHT WILL PLEASE ALL YOUR GUESTS. ITS APPEARANCE
IS AS ELEGANT AS THE 1920S' STYLE OF DRESSING. THIS PUNCH IS A VARIETY
OF VINTAGE, MODERN AND UNIQUE INGREDIENTS COMBINED TO FIT THE
SOPHISTICATED DRINKER.

YIELDS 1 COCKTAIL

---

4 lemons

4 limes

2 c/473 ml white cranberry juice

1 c/200 g raw sugar

6 c/1 l ginger beer

1 750 ml-bottle sparkling wine

6 oz/180 ml peach schnapps

Cut wheels of lemons and limes with a sharp paring knife. Add 30–40 pieces
of ice (or 1½-2 scoops of a 16-ounce/475-milliliter shaker) and the rest of the
ingredients to a large punch bowl and mix with a ladle. Let stand
in the refrigerator for 3 hours.

PRESSED & MINTED

★ ★ ★

AS THE NAME STATES, THIS MIXTURE IS A COMBINATION OF RAW INGREDIENTS.
ONCE PRESSED AND MINTED, SALTY, EARTHY FLAVORS RESULT IN A CLEAN,
COOL COCKTAIL. LET THE MUDDLE BEGIN.

YIELDS 1 COCKTAIL

---

4 mint leaves

½ oz/15 ml simple syrup

1½ oz–2 oz/45–60 ml California rum (we like Agua Libre for this recipe)

½ oz/15 ml St. Germain liqueur

4 oz/120 ml soda water

Ice

Salt for rimming glass

1 lime wedge

Combine mint and syrup in a Tin Play tin. Muddle ingredients so that
the herbs and oils extract from the mint. Add rum, St. Germain and soda water
along with 20 pieces of ice (or 1 scoop of a 16-ounce/475-milliliter shaker).
Shake vigorously and pour into a salted tall collins glass.
Garnish with a wedge of lime.

*We like ours a bit heavy on the rum. When serving to
patrons in a public setting, prepare with 1½ ounce/
45 milliliter of rum. If enjoying this libation at home,
consider the 2-ounce/60 milliliter pour.*

BERGERON'S QUARTER

★ ★ ★

THIS IS THE VIEUX CARRÉ, OR FRENCH QUARTER, POPULARIZED BY
NEW ORLEANS BARTENDER WALTER BERGERON IN THE LATE 1930S. AN
EXCELLENT STAPLE THAT REPRESENTS THE PERSONALITY OF AN ERA.
THE PERFECT COCKTAIL FOR THE PARTY-GOING HISTORIAN!

YIELDS 1 COCKTAIL

¾ oz/22 ml whiskey (we like Jack Daniel's for this recipe)

¾ oz/22 ml cognac

¾ oz/22 ml sweet vermouth (we like Martini & Rossi for this recipe)

⅛ oz Bénédictine liqueur

1 dashe aromatic bitters

1 dash bitters (we like Peychaud's for this recipe)

1 lemon twist for garnish

In a mixing glass, build your cocktail over cracked ice by pouring ingredients
together. Stir for 30 revolutions, strain and pour into a well-chilled coupe.
Garnish with a twist of lemon.

SAGE & SPICE

IT'S COLD, YOUR GUEST WANTS TO STAY FOR A WHILE, WHAT SHALL THEY DRINK? THIS SAVORY, SCARF-UNWRAPPING LIBATION OF COURSE. A TOUCH OF SWEET, A TOUCH OF HEAT AND FULL OF SPICE. GET READY TO PREPARE A SECOND AFTER THE AROMA HITS THE AIR AND NEARBY GUESTS CATCH A SNIFF AND A LOOK.

YIELDS 1 COCKTAIL

---

2 blood orange wheels, 1 for garnish

2 oz/60 ml rye (we like Bulleit for this recipe)

Ice

1 dash AcroAma Tex-Mex Blend

1 oz/30 ml pinot noir (we like Bonterra for this recipe)

1 cinnamon stick for garnish

In a dry Tin Play tin, muddle blood orange and rye. Next add 20 pieces of ice (or 1 scoop of a 16-ounce/475-milliliter shaker), AcroAma Blend, pinot noir and shake for a count of 15. In a large cocktail glass half filled with ice, strain and pour. Garnish with blood orange and cinnamon stick.

ROSE PETAL PUNCH

★ ★ ★

AT FIRST GLANCE, THIS PUNCH IS EASY ON THE EYE AND MAY EVEN HINT
AT FEMININITY, BUT DON'T BE DECEIVED BY THE SEEMINGLY INNOCENT
PARTY SPIRIT; AFTER ALL, IT'S CALLED PUNCH!

YIELDS 8–10 COCKTAILS

THE REFRESHMENT CUBES

6 oz/180 ml gin (we like Cardinal for this recipe)

4 oz/120 ml purified water

**1 small spritz of rosewater hydrosol (we like Mountain Rose for this recipe)
per cube of ice**

2 pink roses, petals torn

In a bar tin, combine gin and purified water. In a standard ice cube tray,
ice mold or silicone ice tray, pour your mixture evenly. Spray a small spritz of
rosewater over each cube and garnish cubes with torn petals. Freeze hours
ahead of time. Can be saved for up to two weeks covered.

*Avoid using tap water because the minerals make the
cubes freeze unevenly and taste bad.*

THE COCKTAIL

Crushed ice

2 750-ml bottles Prosecco D.o.c. di Treviso (we like Mionetto for this recipe)

18 oz/532 ml gin (we like Cardinal for this recipe)

4 sprays rosewater hydrosol (we like Mountain Rose for this resipe)

Rose petals for garnish

Fill a well-chilled punch bowl that has been frozen into a block of ice
or is sitting in ice, one-quarter full of crushed ice. Over ice, slowly pour
Prosecco and gin, stirring as you pour. Once poured into bowl, spray rosewater evenly over punch and stir 4 times. Garnish top of punch and glasses with
roses. Serve in small, stemmed cocktail glasses with ice to be sure
every sip your guest enjoys is crisp.

*Here's where the refreshment cubes come into the mix.
Although your punch is sitting on ice, adding spiked ice
cubes to your punch an hour or two after the party has
started will "re-aestheticize" and refresh.*

ABSINTHE DRIP

★ ★ ★

SERVE UP THIS ONCE-ILLICIT COCKTAIL THE CLASSIC WAY. WITH AN
AESTHETIC THAT WILL NEED LITTLE INTRODUCTION, THE ABSINTHE DRIP
IS A GREAT CONVERSATION STARTER FOR A ROOM FULL
OF NEWLY ACQUAINTED GUESTS.

YIELDS 4 SMALL COCKTAILS

Ice water–filled absinthe fountain (no fountain, no problem, see note below)

1 oz/30 ml absinthe in each glass

1 sugar cube per glass

Fill an absinthe fountain with ice water. Pour absinthe into four absinthe glasses
and place an absinthe spoon topped with 1 sugar cube across the rim. Arrange
glasses under each spigot of the fountain and slowly drip water
over the sugar cube until dissolved and absinthe appears opaque.
Before serving, stir for a count of 5.

*No fountain? While you will only be able to prepare
one at a time, use a pipette to drop ice water evenly
over sugar until cube is dissolved.*

BOURBON CRUSTA

★ ★ ★

THIS MODERN REVIVAL IS YET ANOTHER CHARMING EXCUSE TO DRINK BOURBON AND CRAFT A BEAUTIFUL COCKTAIL FOR GUESTS. BEST ENJOYED IN THE WINTER, IT'S AN EXCELLENT CHOICE TO MAKE AS MINI-COCKTAILS WHILE GUESTS ARE THINKING ABOUT WHAT THEY'D LIKE TO DRINK.

YIELDS 4 SMALL COCKTAILS

---

1 tsp raw sugar for rim dusting

4 lemon twists for garnish

Ice

4 oz/120 ml bourbon (we like Knob Creek for this recipe)

4 dashes aromatic bitters (we like Fee Brothers for this recipe)

4 dashes Orange Curaçao

4 dashes maraschino liqueur (we like Luxardo for this recipe)

4 tsp/20 ml freshly squeezed lemon juice

Before pouring, prepare your mini-cocktail glasses. Dust the rim of 4 sherry glasses with sugar. Place a twist inside the glass so that the pith faces in and the tail sits just above the edge of the glass. To create this miniature party drink, combine ice, bourbon, bitters, Orange Curaçao, maraschino liqueur and juice. Shake well for a count of 20, strain and carefully pour to avoid splash. Guests should enjoy before reaching room temperature.

SUNFIRE PUNCH

★ ★ ★

THE SUNFIRE PUNCH IS FIT FOR ENTERTAINING AT YOUR NEXT
SUMMERTIME FETE. BEST ENJOYED OUTDOORS AND IN WARM WEATHER.
BE PREPARED: THESE PUNGENT YET LIVELY FLAVORS WILL HAVE
ALL YOUR GUESTS ASKING FOR THE RECIPE.

YIELDS 12–15 COCKTAILS

---

1 pt/¼ l fresh orange juice

½ pint/¼ l fresh lemon juice

1 qt/2 l strong black tea

1 qt/2 l rye or blended whiskey

1 750-ml bottle red wine

1 pt/½ l dark rum

½ pt/¼ l brandy

2 oz/60 ml Bénédictine liqueur

1 tbsp/15 ml lemon and/or orange zest

Ice

Twists of lemon peel or oranges for each glass

In a punch bowl, marry all juices and tea. Pour liquor over juice, adding
Bénédictine last and stir. Float zest on top of punch bowl by zesting directly
over punch to express the citrus oils. Wait to add ice to each glass before
serving to be sure punch does not become subdued with water.
Garnish each glass with citrus peels.

MINT JULEP SIPPER

★ ★ ★

LADIES LIKE THE MINT JULEP SIPPER, BUT GUYS, YOU'LL LOVE IT TOO! WE
REALLY LOVE USING ORGANIC HONEY IN THIS SIPPER INSTEAD OF SUGAR.
BECAUSE HONEY BEES ARE ATTRACTED TO A VARIETY OF FLOWERING
CLOVER AND OTHER PLANTS, CHOOSING HONEY REGIONALLY WILL ADD
A SPECIAL ELEMENT OF FLAVOR. YOUR GUESTS WILL LOVE
TO HEAR THIS LITTLE TIDBIT.

YIELDS 1 COCKTAIL

4–5 sprigs of fresh mint, using some for garnish

2 dashes of cherry bitters

2 tsp/10 ml organic raw honey

2 oz/60 ml of bourbon

Ice

Take care to gently muddle a few mint leaves in a bar tin. Nip in your dashes
of bitters, honey and bourbon. Add 20 pieces of ice (or 1 scoop of a
16-ounce/475-milliliter shaker), shake well and serve up with a few mint
leaves for garnish. Sip slowly or this one will go right to your head!

REPEAL DAY

★ ★ ★

"LIPS THAT TOUCH LIQUOR SHALL NOT TOUCH OURS," READ A SIGN IN
PROTEST OF THE REPEAL OF THE 18TH AMENDMENT, ENDING PROHIBITION. WE
OF COURSE WOULD HAVE BURNED THIS SIGN HAD WE SEEN IT! REPEAL DAY,
DECEMBER 5TH, IS NOT ONLY A CELEBRATION FOR THE IMBIBER, BUT ALSO
FOR PURVEYORS OF FINELY CRAFTED DISTILLATIONS AND FERMENTATIONS
THAT WOULD HAVE OTHERWISE BEEN LOST HAD THE BAN NOT BEEN LIFTED!
TELL THAT STORY TO GUESTS AND WATCH THEM TIP THEIR GLASSES TO YOU!

YIELDS 1 COCKTAIL

1 oz/30 ml Scotch whisky (we like Dewar's for this recipe)

½ oz/15 ml Aperol

½ oz/15 ml freshly squeezed blood orange juice

½ oz/15 ml freshly squeezed lemon juice

Ice

1 lemon twist for garnish

In a bar tin, combine Scotch whisky, Aperol and juices with 20 pieces of ice
(or 1 scoop of a 16-ounce/475-milliliter shaker). Shake thoroughly and strain
into a coupe. Garnish with a twist of lemon.

*Dewar's represents the first legal Scotch whisky to arrive
in New York's port once the ban was lifted.*

CHRYSANTHEMUM SIPPER

★ ★ ★

THESE DAYS YOU DON'T HAVE TO HOP ON A BOAT AND LEAVE THE STATES TO
ENJOY THIS SIPPER. IF IT'S YOUR FIRST TIME CRAFTING THIS PROHIBITION-ERA
COCKTAIL OR YOUR GUEST'S FIRST TIME ORDERING, YOU'LL BOTH DISCOVER
PLEASURE WHEN TASTING THIS NOT-TOO-SWEET CLASSIC LIBATION.

YIELDS 1 COCKTAIL

---

4 oz/120 ml dry vermouth (we like Noilly Pratfor this recipe)

2 oz/60 ml Bénédictine liqueur

6 dashes absinthe (we like St. George for this recipe)

Ice

In a mixing glass, stir together vermouth, Bénédictine and absinthe
with 20 pieces of ice (or 1 scoop of a 16-ounce/475-milliliter shaker).
Strain and pour into a well-chilled sipping glass.

CHERRY MAPLE LEAF

★ ★ ★

AUTUMN LEAVES ARE ON THE DOORSTEP AND YOU'RE SERVING GUESTS TO WARM THEIR SPIRITS ON A WINDY DAY. WE LIKE TO THINK OF THE CHERRY MAPLE LEAF AS A COMFORT COCKTAIL—IT WILL GIVE YOU THAT SITTING-BY-THE-FIRE FEEL AFTER A WALK THROUGH THE APPLE ORCHARD.

YIELDS 1 COCKTAIL

---

1 oz/30 ml brandy (we like Rémy Martin for this recipe)

¼ oz/7 ml Maple Syrup

½ oz/15 ml cherry Heering liqueur

¼ oz/7 ml dry vermouth (we like Noilly Prat for this recipe)

3 tsp/15 ml freshly squeezed lemon juice

1 large ice cube or several medium cubes

1 flamed lemon for garnish

1 cinnamon stick

Dash of nutmeg for garnish

In a Boston shaker, combine brandy, maple syrup, cherry Heering, vermouth and juice. Shake well for a count of 20 and pour this comfort cocktail into a handled mason jar with one large ice cube or several medium cubes. Garnish with flamed lemon and cinnamon stick. Dust flame with nutmeg for an extra savory kick.

★ ★ ★

SYRUPS, MIXES & FOAMS

With an abundance of premixed preparations available on the market today, many bartenders balk at the idea of bothering to create their own. While we happily purchase fine preparations ourselves, we really enjoy playing the role of alchemist behind the bar. Syrups, bitters and elixirs are the quintessential elements that allow the bartender versatility in appealing to the sensibilities of each guest. A drop here or there can be a complete game changer not only for a drink, but, more importantly, for the mood of the guest.

You can certainly find some variation of our personal creations, but the joy of creating each syrup, elixir, foam and house mix comes when you see your guest enjoy their first sip with a satisfied expression. Sharing trade secrets is what makes the joy of craft cocktail culture thrive. When one takes special care to create what may define the experience of the guest, it reminds us why we love to entertain.

RHUBARB SYRUP

★ ★ ★

A TART, CRISP FLAVOR TO OFFER BALANCE FOR THE SWEETER COCKTAIL.
FUN TO MAKE AND ENJOY WITH FRIENDS.

YIELDS APPROXIMATELY 8 OZ/240 ML OF SYRUP

2–3 small stalks of chopped rhubarb

1 c/200 g cane sugar

2 c/473 ml water

¼ tsp cinnamon

¼ tsp nutmeg

½ vanilla bean pod

Combine ingredients in a small pot. Bring to a boil, and then reduce heat to a simmer. Simmer 5–7 minutes then let cool completely. Strain ingredients.

Syrup will keep well in fridge covered for two weeks.

HOUSE SAVORY BLOODY MARY MIX

★ ★ ★

ON THE DAY WE MAKE OUR MIX, WE HEAD TO THE FARMERS' MARKET TO
CHOOSE ALL ORGANIC SEASONAL PRODUCE TO CREATE A SPICY AND SA-
VORY MIXTURE GOOD ENOUGH TO ENJOY ON ITS OWN. AS SEASONS CHANGE,
SO DOES THE PRODUCE AVAILABLE FROM LOCALE TO LOCALE. BE SURE TO
CHOOSE TOMATOES THAT ARE FRESH, ORGANIC AND LOCAL TO
YOUR AREA FOR THE BEST RESULT.

YIELD 4 CUPS/1 LITER

---

4 oz/120 ml purified water

8 heirloom tomatoes cored and cut into quarters

3 stalks celery chopped with leaves

½ cucumber chopped

½ c/20 g parsley, finely chopped

1 tsp rainbow peppercorn

1 tsp coriander

1 oz/30 ml kalamata olive juice

1 oz/30 ml freshly squeezed lemon juice

1 oz/30 ml freshly squeezed lime juice

2 dashes salt

2 dashes paprika

2 dashes garlic powder

1 tablespoon raw honey

In a Dutch oven, combine water, tomatoes, celery, cucumber and parsley and
bring to a boil. Reduce heat, cover and simmer for 30 minutes. Remove from
heat. You'll want to put your mixture through a sieve or food mill. A sieve may
take a few more minutes, but we prefer this method. Next, add your remaining
ingredients. Stir for a count of 90, cover and chill. Allow at least
three to five hours to chill before use.

Can be kept refrigerated for one week, unexposed to light.

WHITE CLOUD FOAM

★ ★ ★

WHITE CLOUD FOAM IS IDEAL WHEN THERE'S NOT ENOUGH TIME TO CREATE COCKTAIL FOAM FOR EVERY LIBATION YOU SERVE ON YOUR BAR. IT ISN'T THAT WE'RE SUGGESTING A SHORTCUT PER SE, BUT THE FLAVOR PROFILE IS COMPLEX ENOUGH TO ACT IN A VERSATILE NATURE. SPEAKING OF NATURE, THIS FOAM IS EARTHY YET EXOTIC, SWEET AND A LITTLE SAVORY. PREPARE AHEAD AND KEEP REFRIGERATED UP TO ONE WEEK.

YIELDS APPROXIMATELY 10 SERVINGS

---

8 oz/240 ml organic Thai-style coconut milk or 8 egg whites

5 sprays basil hydrosol (we like Rose Mountain for this recipe)

1 drop ylang-ylang essential oil

1 lemon wedge, juiced

2 tsp/10 ml elderflower liqueur (we like St. Germain for this recipe)

5 tsp/25 ml raw sugar

In your stainless steel whipper, combine Thai-style coconut milk or 8 egg whites with basil hydrosol, ylang-ylang essential oil, juice, elderflower liqueur and raw sugar. Cover, shake well and refrigerate. Voilà.

To make cinnamon foam, just use 1 teaspoon/2.5 grams cinnamon istead of the basil hydrosol.

★ ★ ★

TIPS & TRICKS OF THE TRADE

A personal recommendation is an accommodation any fine bartender is happy to offer. Many a lovely person will sit down at your bar or where you entertain at home without the slightest idea of what to order. Not everyone has "their drink" or even orders the same liquor base every time. But for those who do know what they do, our philosophy is if a patron or guest wishes to drink it, make it for them with a smile—craft it as if it will be the most special cocktail ever to hit their senses. Whether you've got your shirtsleeves rolled up to your elbows, are snappy in suspenders or serve from a white-gloved hand, politeness and personality define bartending with flair. Tell them the story of how their drink came to exist or why you're carefully stirring her drink so it tastes just the way they like it. Mixology and the art of crafting fine cocktails is something to be enjoyed because of the ability to truly bring pleasure and joy to one's social experience.

Many moons ago, after seeing a friend relaxed in front of the same fellow tending bar for a week straight, my friend turned to me and said, "you must think I'm a lush sitting here every day, it's just that this dear man before us can mix a damn good Manhattan. That little thing he does with the cherry and the twist—oh how I love it." Back then, I didn't think much of it, but fast-forward to today—having mixed, muddled, crushed and pressed every leaf, seed and pod my world of herbology offers—I realize a good bartender is just as much an alchemist as an entertainer. And what was that bartender doing with the twist and cherry? He was hand-marinating them in Laphroaig and maple sap for a week ahead of serving. It's all about the tricks of the trade.

PROPERLY CHILLING GLASSWARE

Drinks become classics not only because of their signature mixtures, but also for their aesthetic virtues. An underestimated element that brings together both taste and aesthetics is a properly chilled glass. There is nothing worse than removing a glass from a dishwasher and making a drink for a guest. If they wanted a hot drink, they'd have visited a coffee shop. Every bit of effort you've just made to create your tasty libation will be lost if the appropriate glassware is not at the ideal temperature.

A nearby freezer is by far the best option. Freeze glasses until an opaque layer is visually discernible. If chilling methods are minimal, place glasses on the bar before mixing drinks. Fill with the smallest size of ice available and add soda water. Soda water will accelerate the chilling process for you. Once you've mixed your cocktail, pour ice from the glass, immediately pour and serve the cocktail to your guest, with a napkin of course.

TO SHAKE OR TO STIR

Stirring avoids bruising sensitive ingredients. It's as simple as that. A Manhattan is of course the most popular example of what should never be shaken but only stirred. If you're in doubt, err on the side of stir. Most whiskey creations are stirred. Some might say the same for gin, but as gin cocktails become more complex, shaking is not as looked down upon as it once was. Is there a method to stirring? Well of course! We like to keep it simple—own the bar spoon by firmly grasping between thumb and index and middle fingers. To control the revolutions and be sure that the bowl of your spoon is in charge, remember it's all in the wrist. Keep your hand steady while leading with your wrist.

Tip: without access to a bar tin or mixing glass? A large snifter turned on its side is an ideal vessel for stirring.

THE MUDDLE

The art of the muddle is simple to perfect and as most things go, it comes with experience. It's not necessarily about how often you muddle, yet rather what you muddle. This collection has a vast array of herbs and spices that become kinetic only when muddled. As you muddle each new ingredient, let your nostril be your primary guide. Once aromas hit the air, you're likely done muddling. Are there hard and fast rules? Well, yes. Muddle your softer petals, blooms and leaves with gentle love—it doesn't take much to express their active constituents. For coarser ingredients such as whole dried spices, work in a little elbow grease until their rich aroma fills your nostrils.

The Tin Play Precision Pour Flair tin is our first choice for a premier muddle in almost all cases. When muddling dry, coarse spices, it's nice to have a stone and wooden mortar and pestle on hand.

SMOKE

To decide whether or not to use smoke, it's all about the sought after end result you have in mind for your guest. When we think of smoke, we get happy thinking about our friends mezcal and peat. And when we want to surprise a guest with an unexpected flavor profile for their birthday, we may present them a cocktail with actual smoke instead of candles, go figure. From the barbie to the bar, smoking cocktails is a trick some of your friends and guests will love. For us, we're a mix of foodie, herbalist, alchemist and mixologist, but as far as this trend goes, the purist in both of us wins out. We prefer to create the taste of smoke by torching herbs, salts and syrups on top of wooden boards, and later infusing them into the cocktail.

If you just can't stay away from fire though, we suggest playing around with the Polyscience smoking gun. Easy to procure and handle, you can add a dollop of smoke in a cup, directly into a cocktail or to create a rinse.

If you catch us after hours playing with friends, you might find us preparing a Bell Tower just for fun. Warning: your house or bar may smell more like a hookah lounge than a campfire. You'll need one smoking gun and a bell jar. This technique can be applied for taste to both settle and arouse the spirits and to a myriad of libations.

FAT WASHING

We dig on swine and so will your guests. Adventures in lard is either making you salivate as you read or wanting to jump ahead to the next page. Before you flip, keep in mind that this is not only a hugely popular craft cocktail trend, but a damn tasty technique that opens such liquor as whiskies to a whole new audience of imbibers.

And what fat has the pleasure of being washed? Think salty meats! We've heard about venison and buffalo washes, but bacon will likely gain you the most attention behind the bar.

The process is simple and uncomplicated. Once complete, you have all of the flavor minus the oil and greasiness associated with fat.

To create a whiskey wash with bacon:
Collect the fat of 6 strips of bacon into a heatproof glass container such as Pyrex. Mix 8 ounces/240 milliliters of bourbon (we like Maker's Mark for this recipe) into fat and allow mixture to chill until fat has solidified completely in an airtight container. Once chilled, remove solid fat and strain liquid through a coffee filter into another clean glass container.

Now what? Look to the Whiskey Pig on page 88 to guide your virgin run.

DRIED HERBS, SPICES AND TEAS

Single herbs and spices should be kept sealed in glass jars whenever possible, and teas should be kept in tins. Because some cocktails involve the steeping of tea, do yourself a kind favor by preparing several stainless steel tea balls ahead of time. If your drink takes off by storm, then fill what's appropriate for your guests; but in general, prepare only a few tea balls at a time. Why is this so important? As with herbs, allowing dried teas access to air causes their oils to evaporate, thus risking the diminishment of their taste profile. If you have a signature cocktail that involves crushing or muddling several dry herbs or spices together, it can't hurt to prepare these dry mixtures in tea balls as well.

SELECTING SPIRITS & TASTINGS

In *The Fine Art of Mixing Drinks*, David Embury stresses that a cocktail will never be better than its cheapest ingredients. We agree. The need for high-quality, hand-selected spirits is evermore important when tending to the craft cocktail bar. For those of you tending bar at home, there need not be an exhaustive number of each spirit, but enough of a selection to entice a variety of guests' tastes. The Aero Club, a famous classic cocktail watering hole situated on the border of San Diego's downtown area, boasts a lofty collection of whiskey, bourbon and scotch varieties for patrons to muse over. While this is like candy to a mixologist, a solid lineup of single and double barrel, oak and distilled will offer you liberty to create a vast array of craft cocktails.

Selecting vodka is like a blank canvas before a painter. Choose an acidic vodka to imbue the classic martini of vermouths, twists or olives. Once abhorred in the classic cocktail world, vodka now invites more guests to a bar because it provides versatility. You'll see from our collection how small batch vodka is making a solid play in the modern craft cocktail world.

And what about the apéritif? Apéritifs can be tricky if you haven't tasted many yourself. Take great care when selecting these pre-fete spirits as they can create an overly medicinal taste. Often paired with amuse-bouche, a heavy herbal apéritif may invoke taste bud confusion to a guest or patron, possibly sending them home before making it to the first course.

TESTING YOUR TASTE

You need not be a connoisseur of a thousand spirits to tend a bar with ease and flair. Tasting each spirit you stock in your bar, however, is essential. This may go without saying, but confidence behind the bar is not only honed through a precision pour, but also from a discerning palate. When the opportunity arises, gather friends or other mixologists and invite them to a tasting in your home or get out and try what's new.

And for those of you who love to create fine craft cocktails and entertain but are not a lover of the drink taste yourself, you can still fully participate in tasting, for it involves far more sensitivity beyond the tip of your tongue and mouthfeel. Ever engaged in wine tasting activities? Create this practice with all of your libations.

Try this: Pour just two or three drops into a glass appropriate to the libation you will be tasting. Swirl the spirit in the glass just under your nose and inhale deeply. Now set it down. Ask yourself, "Do I smell hints of anise? Is that a smoky aroma?" Pick up that glass and give it a second swirl. By now that initial hint of smoky anise may have opened to reveal nutmeg, caramel and earthy moss. Never underestimate the subtle power of inhalation.

Also, give the "almost taste" a try. After that second swirl, swirl again at mouth level with your mouth open, tongue gently resting on your bottom lip and slowly breathe in the aromas through your mouth. Another trick to discern elements of mouthfeel and finish.

THE RINSE

Guests love watching mixologists prepare their libations before them. Preparing a drink with a rinse is a polite way to spike your guest's drink with an otherwise unexpected flavor profile. When a drink calls for a rinse, prepare the glass for the guest to see . . . and smell. When poured into the proper glassware, the scent of the rinse will heighten your guest's senses and interest. It all adds to the effect of entertaining while offering a well-balanced cocktail.

The method is to swirl liquor around in the glass until the entire inside is coated. You'll want to pour out any excess. Or, if it's that kind of party, you can pour the excess into your guest's mouth. Serving in a bar? Politely discard the excess. Be sure to avoid splash.

Note: The Vig (page 98) is a fine example of the rinse.

TOOLS

Every bartender comes to love a few tools that define the style in which they create signature cocktails. To prepare classic cocktails, there exist special tools you'll want to procure.

Bar Spoon: No matter whose bar you're at, in whatever country, a bar spoon delivers a standardized measurement to ensure a well-mixed drink every time. The bar spoon is ideal as it doubles for a stir stick long enough to prepare drinks mixed into pitchers. When measuring, one bar spoon is equivalent to 1 teaspoon.

Strainer & Sieve: Your bar is likely to already have a strainer. Good. But a sieve, perhaps not. Craft cocktails ask for fine ingredients that will muddy a drink if not extracted before serving. A small, fine sieve is a mixologist master's best friend behind the bar!

ICE

"Ice and more ice," is the advice that any bartender passes on to the next generation of bartenders. But does it need be as fancy as pop culture would like us to think? Ice is the element that determines the mood of all drinks, so what it needs to be is the right size and shape to create the desired mouthfeel and consistency. With larger cubes (or spheres) and therefore surface area, even melting ensues. To consistently create simple cubes at home, choose filtered water for a more even freeze.

Snow Ice: Snow ice, mostly used in juleps and mojitos, is created by placing ice in a Lewis bag and hammering away with a mallet. Of course, this can create quite the racket, but, then again, so does a blender.

Cracked Ice: It goes without saying that cracked ice is ideal for cooling cocktails while smaller, finer pieces of ice are for diluting. To crack like a polite pro, we suggest using a lint-free towel wrapped around a cube of ice and grasped in one hand. In your opposing hand, hold the very end of the handle of a twisted bar spoon and with the flick of your wrist, once, twice and thrice, crack away at the covered cube. This is the technique we enlist for Manhattan making.

Large Cubes and Spheres: There are three purposes for large cubes and spheres: to cool cocktails more evenly, to avoid dilution of spirits, and to infuse with flowers or special ingredients that will build flavor and aesthetic appeal of the drink.

Dry Ice Pellets: Dry ice, when aptly handled and reserved for special occasions, can appeal to the eye and the senses. Dry ice deserves a practice run before serving to guests so you don't leave them and their drink up in smoke. Because it can cause frostbite, be sure to practice proper etiquette by placing dry ice into drinks with ice tongs. When serving a single drink, all you'll need are one or two dry ice chips.

BAR TINS, SHAKERS AND CRYSTAL GLASS FOR MIXING

Some of you are practical and some of you are lovers of trendy design. Whatever you decide to create your cocktail in, keep in mind the type of cocktail you're building, whether it will require a muddle, if it shall be stirred or shaken, its temperature and if straining is required.

Our choice? Keep one of each on hand.

Tin Play Precision Pour Flair Tins: We certainly have an affection for the durable and aesthetically pleasing Tin Play Precision Pour Flair tin. With a precise muddling and measuring tool, this all-in-one allows the at-home mixologist an opportunity to experiment with a vast array of recipes with confidence. Guests will also love to watch you build, shake and pour from this modern tin.

Boston Shaker: For smaller, exceptionally cold cocktails, a traditional Boston shaker bar tin comes in handy. It guarantees proper dilution and is simple to handle.

Crystal Mixing Glasses: And for that Manhattan, a crystal glass of course. The glass provides "temperature insurance," which is why we build all martinis in this vessel. Beautiful to view and relaxing to create; a lovely addition to any craft cocktail bar.

Atomizers, Pipettes & Hydrosols: Some bartenders think atomizing is just nonsense because it resembles spraying perfume. For something as expensive as an absinthe or an aged whiskey, you just might want to stretch the expense to an atomizer to prevent waste. Our preferences are amber bottles and pipettes. Perhaps it's the mad scientist in us, or that we want all of the booze to infuse into the cocktail, but we prefer droppers over atomizers—they're easier to handle and more precise.

What do guests love? Well, both. Bartending with a touch of flair would seem parallel to featuring an atomizer at one's bar, but the experienced drinker of well-balanced classic cocktails may simply see this as gimmicky. If you command your libations especially well with the atomizer, then own it and let guests know why you love it.

Hyrdosols are a favorite among mixologists. Offering an excellent finish to a drink is the stuff hydrosols are made of. What remains apart from the essential oil of an herb, plant or spice and which contains active medicinal, food-grade constituents is bottled and prepared to be sprayed. We could not possibly offer guests half of our originally created libations without this nifty and practical invention.

OTHER BAR TOOLS TO CREATE EASE AND AESTHETIC APPEAL

Hawthorne and Julep Strainers: These provide precision straining for cocktails such as the Manhattan.

Bar Pins for Garnishing: While toothpicks will do in a pinch, bar pins offer an artistic, aesthetic visual to your cocktail.

Jiggers for Measuring: If you're just getting started behind the bar, it's always nice to provide guests with a precise pour.

Peelers, Zesters, Graters and Microplaners. These are must-haves for the many shapes and sizes these recipes call for.

Ice Molds: Preparing your own circular ice balls was never easier with handy silicone ice molds. Easy to infuse with flowers or make simple cubes, every guest is sure to love the shape.

Sharp Knives: There is only one kind of knife to have behind the bar and that's a sharp one. Dull knives not only yield inconsistent garnishes, but they're also a hazard to the bartender's safety.

Juicers: A simple glass juicer is great for making more than one drink.

Lint-Free Bar Towels: These keep you and your glassware spot free, and your guests from drinking lint.

OUR FAVORITE BRANDS

In step with choosing just the right spirits to delight our guest's tastes, we love the signature flavors of several special syrups, oils, hydrosols and bitters. Royal Rose syrups, NHR Organic Oils, Fee Brothers bitters, Urban Moonshine bitters, Mountain Rose organic hyrdosols and Simply Organic oils are named exclusively throughout our recipes as our favorites behind the bar. We've chosen to highlight these exceptional accompaniments because their ingredients are pure and unadulterated, rendering what we think is the perfect cocktail.

GARNISHES & ACCOMPANIMENTS

While the right tools are essential to constructing any cocktail, garnishes and accompaniments are what create a more noteworthy, lingering memory of, "I'm going to order that next time." Guests will recall the floating hibiscus flower or neroli orange–infused foam before recalling the name of the drink and are sure to make second requests for their favorite, aesthetically pleasing cocktail.

We've hand-selected our favorite, most versatile garnishes and accompaniments.

While many garnishes can be refrigerated for a short period of time, we suggest market fresh, organic fruits, herbs, roots, vegetables and flowers whenever possible. Infusions infuse because fresh herbs are packed with essential oils, and ginger snaps because it's just been peeled. If it's not in season, think adventurously—a pomegranate old-fashioned can always transform into one with boysenberry.

Citrus: Choose fresh, firm citrus to ensure oils have not been expressed. Citrus on the branch with leaves and flowers intact should be considered a score. Don't pass these up because flowers can be substituted for essential oils by being pressed with your mortar and pestle.

Flowers: Pick what's just unfurling. Best purchased the morning of entertaining and kept in a cool, aerated area with stems submerged in warm water. Look for organic edible varieties such as roses, violets, forget-me-nots and marigolds.

Herbs: Herbs that are firm, velvety and filled with aroma are best for cocktails. Rub a section of sprig or leaf between your fingers—if the scent remains on your fingertips, choose these. Unless you're preparing drinks that call for blooms, avoid herbs that have begun to flower. This indicates the herb is ready for seed and less than appropriate for cocktails. It may also reveal a bitter plant. Herbs are heartiest when refrigerated or kept in a short glass of water.

Olives: Hand stuff your own fresh green olives with both sharp and blue cheeses, marinated nuts, pickles and European peppers. Our favorite? Spanish Manchego cheese and Marcona almond stuffed on the day of entertaining. No time to stuff? Try Filthy Food's pickle-stuffed olives created by brothers Daniel and Marc Singer.

Vegetables: Fresh, crisp and just been picked from the market are always best. If you'll be pickling your own garnishes, try green beans, cucumbers, carrots and beets.

Dry Spices & Herbs: Building this selection may take time. If a full bar setup is your goal, review your seasonal cocktail menu, then get to list making. Organic spices and herbs are of course the best—they are unadulterated and the essential oils and the active constituents are left intact. Choose bulk organic spices and herbs if you'll be crafting often. To start your collection, here are the spices and herbs we can't go without:

• Borage flowers
• Caraway
• Cinnamon stick
• Coriander
• Fennel
• Lavender petals
• Powdered chili
• Powdered nutmeg
• Rainbow peppercorns
• Saffron
• Sea salt
• Whole and powdered cardamom
• Whole dried chilis
• Whole star anise

Teas: Loose leaf tea is ideal as it allows you to play with the strength of steep and yield without creating waste. Choose organic tea leaves whenever possible. Best stored in dry tins and glass containers.

Coffees: A must-have behind any bar. Choose two types to have on hand, one being a smokier grind to mix with bourbon and brandy cocktails. Choose beans if you have a grinder and if not, choose finely ground espresso. Store in dry tins or glass containers. Keep in a cool, dark area.

Marinated Cherries: Prepare your own. You'll feel accomplished and your guests will be thrilled. Having savored your own creation will allow you to create even more precise flavor profiles as cherries vary in taste depending upon what part of the season they have been picked.

MARINATED CHERRY RECIPE

★ ★ ★

1 lb/454 g dark, pitted cherries

16 oz/473 ml brandy (we like Rémy Martin for this recipe)

2 oz/60 ml sweet vermouth (we like Carpano Antica for this recipe)

Fill a glass jar with cherries, cover with brandy and vermouth.

Store in a cool, dark location for six weeks.

RESOURCES

Tins
Tin Play Precision Pour Flair Tins
5967 Gaines Street
San Diego, CA 92110
858.337.8816
www.tinplay.com

Amber Glass Bottles with Pipettes
Far East Summit
P.O. Box 545
Pleasant Hill, OR 97455
888.441.0489
www.fareastsummit.com/home.html

Raw Chinese Herbs & Teas
Kamwo Herbal Pharmacy
(tell Anthony we sent you)
211 Grand Street
NY, NY 10013
212.966.6370
www.kamwo.com

Artisinal Cocktail Pickles
Filthy Foods
221 Conover Street
Brooklyn, New York 11231
877.834.5849
www.filthyfood.com

Cherries
Luxardo Marasca Cherries
www.luxardo.com

Hydrosols, Herbs & Spices
Frontier Organic Co-Op
Frontier Natural Products Co-op
PO Box 299
3021 78th Street
Norway, IA 52318
800.669.3275
www.frontiercoop.com

AcroAma Organic Blends
124 N. Commerce Street
Galena, IL 61036
563.552.7415
www.acroamablends.com

BITTERS

Fee Brothers Bitters
453 Portland Avenue
Rochester, NY 14605
585.544.9530
www.feebrothers.com

Urban Moonshine
1 Mill Street, Suite 110
Burlington, VT 05401
802.428.4707
www.urbanmoonshine.com

Food Grade Essential Oils
NHR Organic Oils
Dept AA566
P.O. Box 618001
Dallas, TX 75261
866.816.0195
www.nhrorganicoils.com

**Vintage Bar Supplies, Rare Liquors
& Specialty Glassware for the
Professional & Home Bar**
Bar Keeper
3910 W. Sunset Boulevard
Silver Lake, CA 90029
323.669.1675
www.barkeepersilverlake.com

ACKNOWLEDGMENTS

To our delight, we are happy to thank those whose efforts signify and symbol-ize the very expression of this collection. Thank you to our nearest and dearest family and friends for your enthusiasm, encouragement, personal anecdotes and especially for not scolding us for keeping the oddest of hours while bringing this project together—ahem, Danielle and Steve.

Mr. Sean Cassidy, proprietor of Cassidy Images, thank you for your unwavering support to create photos that make our readers want to imbibe and imbibe some more! Your special brand of humor puts a smile on our faces, and we love the fun polaroid camera you brought to our shoots to capture the mood of the day. Thank you for being at the ready and sharing those odd hours we kept!

To our generous hosts who invited us into their craft cocktails domains to create the photos that grace these pages, we are forever grateful for your generosity. San Diego's Aero Club, owned since 2004 by Bay Ridge, Brooklyn, native Bill Lutzius. The Aero Club now boasts 600-plus whiskies, more than any bar in San Diego. The Aero Club has been named one of America's top dive bars by Maxim magazine. A special thanks to lifelong friend, business partner and expert spirit guide, GM, Chad Berkey of the Aero Club. Your vivacious, at-attention, ready-to-go-ness is the stuff bartending with flair is made of. A true icon in the making, we thank you for both your hard, roll-up-your sleeves work and being an exemplary model for infusing authenticity into your craft. Having said that, thank you to Tin Play Precision Pour Flair Tins for making the creations on these pages possible for our professional colleagues and friends at home. Prohibition, one of San Diego's first underground revivals of speakeasy culture—we remember when a list and a knock on the door was required to enter! Thank you to proprietor, Nicholas Tomasello and master mixologist Shawn Burkholder for making our early morning experience come to life. We can't wait to put on some sparkles and stop in for a libationary visit.

A big thanks to Brian Malarkey and the very professional staff at Searsucker San Diego for hosting what turned out to be one the most fun shoots during your busy brunch run. Thank you so very much for serving us coffee. Our hats go off to Fausto David Esquivel for being so darn sweet. Thank you for your extension of help, loaning us your personal bar tools and epitomizing what matters most about this book—keeping the tradition of true mixologist manners alive. Can't wait for you to light something on fire for us! Thanks go to Matt Hoyt of Starlite for inviting us to shoot in your architectural god of a craft cocktail bar. How we loved walking through that unforgettable doorway—truly a timeless San Diego fixture you've created. The fine gentlemen who own and operate the oh so unique art-adorned walls of San Diego's Lion's Share, Roy Ledo and Hassan Mahmood—thank you for personally taking part in the creation of our shoots.

A special thanks to our double feature, mixologist and model, Matt Kukral of San Diego's Cucina Urbana, who honed his skills, becoming one of San Diego's finest mixologists with over 8½ years in the business. You will be a go-to spirit advisor for any future projects. The lovely and talented Ashley Smithey for your fine virtues of suspending the aesthetics of classic cocktail in time, just long enough to create a modern feel, thank you for offering us your personal trademark style both in craft and culture. Mr. Sean Mattix, thank you for always supporting our every endeavor, for being our friend, offering us opportunities that have helped us see our professional goals through and of course that uncanny, kid-trickery you're always up to!

To our publisher, editor and designer, Will, Marissa and Meg at Page Street Publishing for presenting such a fun project and extending us creative vision, thank you. And thanks to Elerey LeBlanc for keeping up with his pool game so that we could be introduced to Will in the first place! A special thanks to our collaborator at Garden Eats, Kath Dionese, for being our in-house herb whisperer—your expertise breathed life into some of our signature flavor profiles. Laura Seery and Livia Manfredi, your culinary know-how, love of creating the written word and landmarks as true cultivators of memorable social experiences have helped create visions that no writer's block could stand up to.

Thank you to masters of the herbal world at PCOM San Diego, Mr. Warren Sheir and Tan Tan Huang for making the nuances and subtleties of herbal pharmacology become tangible through fun anecdotes, personal stories and Chinese food therapy field trips to the market. Jess McCalister, secret agent, liaison lady—thank you for your brainstorming session amidst your oh-so-busy and bustling agenda! To our friends and colleagues in the entertainment and food world, Carissa Giacalone, Denny Walsh, Magnus Mumby, Tejal Rao, Scott Leibfried, Devin Parr, Terri Neuwerth, Michael Blaise Kelly and Jennifer McCray, thank you for asking authentic questions about our project, for you were once in our shoes, organizing, writing, shooting, crafting, cooking. Your stamp of public approval on this project means the world to us— we thank you for loving our work and introducing it to your friends, families, audiences, guests and students.

AUTHORS

★   ★   ★

Jeremy LeBlanc began his bartending career at one of Boston's busiest and most prominent clubs, The Rack, and today is the president of Tin Play Precision Pour Flair Tins, LLC. Jeremy complements Tin Play with more than 15 years of experience as a bartender and as an active member of the downtown San Diego community. Jeremy helped Altitude Sky Lounge (Condé Nast pick for top 10 rooftop bar's in the world), become a huge success in the San Diego nightlife scene. He currently serves as Altitude's master mixologist.

Christine Dionese is a seasoned food, health and lifestyle writer with a flair for bringing the most unlikely flavor profiles together. Drawing on her deep-rooted scientific prowess in molecular herbology, botany and food science, Christine brings the natural elements of the garden, farmer's market and test kitchen together at the bar. Christine is the co-founder of Garden Eats, an organic kitchen gardening outfit purveying specialty medicinal organic foods, techniques and molecular beverage creation for modern living. Ask her of her favorite muse, and she will reply, "creating such memorable experiences they can be tasted when recalled and talked about."

INDEX

★ ★ ★